LESSONS FROM A CHRISTMAS TREE FARM

LESSONS FROM A CHRISTMAS TREE FARM

◆

A Devotional and Study Guide Resource

Michael D. Kurtz, D. Min.

iUniverse, Inc.
New York Lincoln Shanghai

LESSONS FROM A CHRISTMAS TREE FARM
A Devotional and Study Guide Resource

iUniverse, Inc.

For information address:
iUniverse, Inc.
2021 Pine Lake Road, Suite 100
Lincoln, NE 68512
www.iuniverse.com

Unless otherwise noted, the version of scripture used is: NIV

Cover design by Joanna Stanton

ISBN: 0-595-33225-0 (pbk)
ISBN: 0-595-66782-1 (cloth)

Printed in the United States of America

Contents

HARVESTING

PROLOGUE

For nearly twenty years I worked part-time raising and tending Christmas trees in the high country of North Carolina. This horticulture endeavor provided not only a therapeutic, out-of-doors-outlet, but also proved to be an avenue of analogies for life lessons.

The instructions from God's creation are pronounced and profound if we will open our eyes, minds, and hearts to the inherent lessons. Growing Christmas trees, like growing in the Christian faith, is neither quick nor easy. There is required of us patience, diligence, and hard work. And, above all, divine grace.

When I started planting the first crop of Christmas trees during the autumn of 1979 I never envisioned the journey of experiences, relationships, and lessons that lay ahead for me. The following pages relate a portion of those "tree teachings".

THIS BOOK IS LOVINGLY DEDICATED TO MY FAMILY AND TO MY ASHE COUNTY FAMILY—A PEOPLE AND A PLACE I SHALL ALWAYS CALL HOME.—WHICH ONLY GOES TO PROVE "YOU CAN TAKE THE BOY FROM THE MOUNTAINS, BUT YOU CANNOT TAKE THE MOUNTAINS FROM THE BOY."

PLANTING

1

A VISION

Proverbs: "Without a vision the people perish." (Proverbs 29:18, KJV).

I don't know what possessed me. I had no experience in growing Christmas trees. I had no connections. I had no extra capital. I did not even own any land.

But I had an idea. My mind entertained a vision. I wanted to start a small Christmas tree farm. This avocation would provide a way of working out-of-doors in God's nature, which has always been a love of mine. It would provide a way of tending the "garden" in which we have been placed. In addition, the trees at harvest time would provide a good source of income for future expenses and investments.

One afternoon, in the coaches office at the high school where I taught, I shared my "Christmas tree dream" with two other teachers. They listened. They were interested. But, naturally they wanted some time to think about this possibility.

Three days later they were on board! So, in 1979 we began formulating a plan. We would consult with the local agricultural extension agent. We would inquire as to how to obtain the fraser fir seedlings needed for planting. And, my parents would graciously permit us to use some of their land upon which to plant the trees. This property was located in a community named "Buffalo". So, we would call our enterprise the "Buffalo Fir Christmas Tree Farm".

The "Christmas Tree Dream" became a reality. The dream mandated hours and hours of careful planning, hard work, persistent attention to the trees, and continual learning as to the best methods of tree growing and care. A large amount of time, energy, and commitment was required. Yet, the events, experiences, and lessons that this realized vision provided far surpassed the physical and fiscal investments and benefits.

Following this vision enabled me to focus time and energy upon a worthwhile goal and project; involved me in some great relationships with some very special persons; inspired me as I observed, and help nurture, the growth of God's natural world; and, encouraged me as I watched a dream materialize.

It's true—without a vision we perish. A vision, a dream, gives us purpose and direction. A vision keeps us moving forward.

The Australian coat of arms pictures two creatures—the emu, a flightless bird, and the kangaroo. The animals were chosen because they share a characteristic that appealed to the Australian citizens. Both the emu and the kangaroo can move only forward, not back. The emu's three-toed foot causes it to fall if it tries to go backwards, and the kangaroo is prevented from moving in reverse by its large tail.

In following God's vision for our lives, we can learn lessons from the emu and the kangaroo—moving only forward, never back by God's good grace!

PRAYER: O God, place within me your vision for my life. I need your direction and wisdom so that I will be pleasing to you and encouraging to others. Open not only my mind and heart to your vision for my days, but also open my hands that I may do your will. For our Lord's sake. Amen.

QUESTIONS AND REFLECTIONS

1. What is your God-directed vision for life?

2. If you have never done so, take several minutes to write down a vision statement for your life.

3. What does the Bible mean when it says: "Without a vision the people perish"?

4. Think of some visionaries that you have heard about or that you personally know. What characteristics and qualities do they possess? How might these qualities be more evident in your life?

2

TEAMWORK

Ecclesiastes 4:9,10: "Two are better than one, because they have a good return for their work. If one falls down, his friend can help him up. But pity the man who falls and has no one to help him up."

Our project began with three teachers and three-thousand trees. From the outset teamwork was our mode-of-operation. I could never have been successful at growing Christmas trees without my partners—fellow school teachers Sam and Larry.

In all our years of working together three essential qualities of teamwork standout: trust, cooperation, and hard work. We trusted each other. We did not make business decisions without first conferring with one another. We cooperated as a team of three. We did not always agree with one another. But, we would always discuss and listen until there was consensus. And, we spent many long days working side-by-side in the Christmas tree fields.

For nearly twenty years Sam and Larry and I were partners in this "cottage" business of growing Christmas trees. Yet, we were more than partners. We became good friends. To this day theses men remain supportive friends in my life.

In the book of Ecclesiastes (4:9,12) King Solomon writes: "Two people can accomplish more than twice as much as one…Three are even better (than two), for a triple-braided cord is not easily broken."

From the very beginning humanity was not intended to be alone. We need each other. Great things can be accomplished when groups of friends work together with a common focus and purpose.

Allow me to illustrate this teamwork principle through one mid-Western farmer's life:

Herman Ostry's barn floor was under 29-inches of water because of a rising creek. The Bruno, Nebraska farmer invited a few friends to a "barn raising." He needed to move his entire 17,000 pound barn to a new foundation more than 143 feet away. His son Mike devised a lattice work of steel tubing, and nailed, bolted, and welded it on the inside and the outside of the barn. Hundreds of handles were attached.

After one practice lift, 344 volunteers slowly walked the barn up a slight incline, each supporting less than fifty pounds. In just three minutes, the barn was on its new foundation.

With God's help we can accomplish great things when we work together—practicing cooperation and teamwork.

God never intended that his children would live like hermits. He intended that they would interact…that they would help one another along the journey of life—loving one another, encouraging one another, admonishing one another, hugging one another, picking one another up when falls occur, rejoicing together and weeping together.

Two people can accomplish more than twice as much as one. And, as a wise king reminds us: "They get a better return for their labor…"

We were not created to be independent islands of self-sufficiency. We were made to relate, to interact and to support each other.

In fact, Ecclesiastes reminds us: "A person standing alone can be attacked and defeated."

Standing alone is awfully despairing, and it's dangerous. If I may get personal with you—Do you have a few people in your life who really know you? Are you accountable to anybody for the way you live? Or, are you just trying to go the distance all alone?

Loneliness, standing alone, the writer of Ecclesiastes says leads to being attacked and defeated. We need to avoid isolationism like the plague.

Isolationism leads to defeat. Mark it down. You simply cannot cover all sides where the enemies attack. There is nothing quite like a trusted friend to help you make it through a hard time. For, it is written, "Two can stand back-to-back and conquer."

Interestingly, in the Bible, when Jesus refers to the Holy Spirit as "Helper", he uses a Greek word, "paraclete",—an ancient warrior's term.

Greek soldiers went into battle in pairs. So, when the enemy attacked, they could draw together back-to-back, covering each other's blind side. One's battle partner was the "paraclete."

Teamwork is far better than isolationism. "Two people can accomplish more than twice as much as one and they get a better return for their labor." Solomon goes on to say, "Three are even better (than two), for a triple-braided cord is not easily broken."

Think about a braid. A braid appears to contain only two strands of hair. But it is impossible to create a braid with only two strands. If the two could be put together at all, they would quickly unravel.

Herein lies the mystery: What looks like two strands requires a third. The third strand, though not immediately evident, keeps the strands tightly woven.

"Three is even better." How true this proved to be as I reflect upon the years of teamwork and friendship in the Christmas tree fields with Sam and Larry. We were able to come alongside one another and stand together through the challenges and changes on a Christmas tree farm by maintaining comradeship and cooperation.

PRAYER: O Eternal Presence, how grateful we are that we are not alone! We are gifted with your holy and powerful presence through your Holy Spirit. Nothing can separate us from your love in Christ Jesus.

We also praise you for the family and friends you have placed in our life journey so that we are not isolated. Enable us to open our life to others' help and friendship so that we may be a better friend to others along the way. In the name of the greatest Friend we pray, Amen.

QUESTIONS AND REFLECTIONS

1. Call to mind three or four friends who have been there for you in your journey of life. Possibly this would be a good moment to write them or call them or see them and thank them for their gift of friendship.

2. Read Ecclesiastes 4:9,10 and relate what this passage says to you about friendship.

3. "Two are better than one, because they have a good return for their work." (Ecc. 4:9). One of the great benefits and joys of friendship is teamwork. In what ways are you being a "team player" in the home, on t he job, at your church, etc.?

4. True and trusted friends are not easy to find. Not every one can be our friend, nor can we be close friend with every one else. A trusted, authentic friend is a blessed gift from God. Read Proverbs 18:24 and discuss why every one cannot, and should not, be our friend.

5. Locate the following scripture passages and reflect upon what each says about friendship:

Proverbs 17:17	Ruth 1:16
Proverbs 27:10	II Timothy 1:16
Proverbs 27:17	Acts 2:42
John 15:13	I John 1:7
I Samuel 18:1	Philippians 1:3

3

A SEED BECOMES A TREE

"The kingdom of heaven is like a mustard seed, which a man took and planted in his field. Though it is the smallest of all your seeds, yet when it grows, it is the largest of garden plants and becomes a tree, so that the birds of the air come and perch in its branches"—Jesus (Matthew 13, 31,32).

Christmas trees begin their life in a nursery. Here, seeds are taken from the cones of mature trees, planted and covered with straw. In addition, they are covered with shade cloth to prevent them from being damaged by frost or sun. After about three years, the fraser fir seedlings are ready to be moved to the line-out beds for further growing.

Fascinating! Miraculous! Contained in a tiny, seemingly insignificant seed is the origin and life of a large, stately tree! Without the seed there would be no tree. Talk about great things coming in small packages!

Our culture and era is very impressed with big and large. Sometimes we think "the bigger, the better." And, the big, stately Christmas trees are impressive! Nothing inherently wrong with big. Big is not necessarily bad. Yet, neither is small necessarily bad.

But the potential danger in glamorizing the big is to miss out on the necessity and beauty of the small.

As I write these words I am returning home by plane from a Christian leadership institute hosted by a mega-church on the West coast. This mega-church had invited well-known pastors from large churches to share their stories with us. I found these pastors' stories very inspiring and informative.

Yet, what I also found inspiring was a presentation on the third day of this four-day training event. It was given by a middle-age, single-mother, pastor of a congregation similar in size to what most of us in attendance pastored. Her's was a dynamic, growing congregation, but in contrast to the mega churches, would not even be considered a large church. This pastor's presentation reminded me of the importance and relevance of every church, large and no so large!

In fact, in all of Christendom there are no small churches! There are some small-membership churches maybe, but never a small church because we are all part of the Body of Christ. The Body of Christ is universal. The true, divine church of Jesus Christ supersedes humanly devised and divided denominations. The true church of Christ is an organism more than an organization.

How could we label that which is universal and unified as "small"? "Small church" is an oxymoron. "Small" and "church" do not fit together. There are large-membership churches and small-membership churches. Yet, all are part of the same family. There are unique differences and special ministries of each congregation, no matter the size, that are needed for ministry in and to the world.

The secret to an abundant and fulfilling life, whether congregation or individual, is to bloom where you are planted. A tree does not start off as a tree. A tree always begins as a tiny seed. Even after a year of being in the nursery the fraser fir is a seedling only the size of a quarter. There is required many more years of growth before the tree becomes large enough for its intended purpose.

Transformation includes small seeds becoming large trees. St. Paul in writing a letter to the first-century Christians in Corinth says: "I planted the seeds, Apollos watered, but it is God who provided the growth…"

A sincere faith dedicated to God will result in incredible growth. God will take the small and broken mess that we bring and through His mercy and grace transform that offering into something multiplied and whole.

Hundreds of years ago a young Hebrew boy saw a need and he approached Jesus and offered him the little bit of food he possessed—five loaves of bread and two fish. And through the miraculous love and power of God, Jesus multiplied that small, insignificant offering into a fantastic feast that fed thousands of folk!

Seeds do become trees! May we never forget the power and potential of small steps, small acts of kindness, and tiny seeds. One minister reflects:

"To give my life for Christ appears glorious. To pour myself out for others…to pay the ultimate price of martyrdom—I'll do it. I'm ready, Lord, to go out in a blaze of glory.

We think giving our all to the Lord is like taking a $1,000 bill and laying it on the table—"Here's my life, Lord, I'm giving it all."

But the reality for most of us is that he sends us to the bank and has us cash in the $1,000 for quarters. We go through life putting out 25 cents here and 50 cents there. Listen to the neighbor kid's troubles instead of saying, "Get lost." Go to a committee meeting. Give a cup of water to a shaky old man in a nursing home.

Usually giving our life to Christ isn't glorious. It's done in all those little acts of love, 25 cents at a time. It would be easy to go out in a flash of glory; it's harder to live the Christian life little by little over the long haul.

PRAYER: Miracle-working God, it is so easy to get caught up in the big that we fail to see the significant in the small. It is so tempting to become swept away by the impressiveness of large numbers that we miss the specialness of each one. Help us to appreciate the big and celebrate the small. May we be reminded that big and small—all belong to your kingdom. Through Christ we pray, Amen.

QUESTIONS AND REFLECTIONS

1. Read Matthew 10:42 and discuss the importance of "a cup of cold water" ministry.

2. Discuss the biological principle of seed germination. Reflect upon the life that is contained within a tiny seed. Study Matthew 13:31-33. In what ways does the biological principle of germination apply to spiritual growth?

3. Locate John 5:1-14—The Feeding of the Five Thousand. Attempt to put yourself in the place of the young boy with the five loaves and two fish. What are your thoughts? What are your feelings?

4. Most of our days and most of our character is shaped by so-called small, ordinary, everyday experiences. Rather than $1,000 dollars during a one-time experience, life seems rather numerous exchanges of 25 cents. How does this "quarter quest" square with your life and with your philosophy of living?

5. We can miss so much throughout our life because we are looking for something "big" or fantastic, when all along those small things inevitably bring meaning and joy to our days. What are you missing in your day-to-day life, or taking for granted, while dreaming of some fantastic future event or experience?

4

NURTURED IN THE NURSERY

"The best place to find a helping hand may very well be at the end of one's wrist. But there are times when it's necessary to help someone find that hand by holding it for a while."—Anonymous

I once heard it said that I Corinthians15:51 should be placed above the door of every church nursery. The verse reads: "We shall not all sleep. But we shall be changed in a moment, in the twinkling of an eye..."

That's pretty descriptive of some days in a nursery. And, it's good news because a nursery is a place where little ones are to be cared for and tended to. A nursery is to be like an intensive care unit of sorts where the babies are fed and changed and entertained and hopefully rocked to sleep. It is a place where tender loving care is delivered to each child.

A nursery is a place of total dependency. That's why intensive care is required. Little babies are helpless and dependent upon the nursery workers for their every need. They need to spend some significant time in the nursery before they are ready to graduate to a more independent level of functioning.

Fraser fir trees spend the first three years of their life in the nursery. It is here they are protected. It is here they find security. It is here they are nurtured from seed to seedling. Upon a good start and stay in the nursery, after three years, the seedling will be able to be more independent. The seedling is then planted outside the nursery in a line-out bed, alongside other seedlings of comparable size and age.

There are times in our life when we all need the nurturing care of an intensive care unit—a time(s) for our friends, family and church family to place supportive, non-judgmental, unconditional loving arms around us...Helping us recover until we can put our feet on the ground and go forward once again.

I affirm that the church should serve as an intensive care unit for wounded souls! Jesus said, "I did not come to heal the whole…but the sick and lost." Jesus' mission, mandate, purpose, and ministry was to bring healing and wholeness. Jesus' mission is to be our mission. Christians are to be nurturing-nursery-workers and intensive-care-unit-technicians reaching out to the least, the lost, and the lonely.

And, then, once we reach out to these persons we need to invite them in…to become part of God's family and Christ's church. We are nurtured by God and others so that we might nurture and disciple others in the faith.

You cannot work in a Christmas tree nursery without getting your hands dirty. There is required digging in, and working with, the dirt in order to have healthy, growing trees.

Additionally, you do not grow Christmas trees vicariously. Growing Christmas trees is very much a hands-on project. You don't grow the trees from a distance. They demand contact. They require TLC.

Nurturing persons, especially new Christians in the faith, also mandates that we get our hands dirty and have a hands-on approach to our relationships. Disciples of Christ are not nurtured nor grown from a distance. Loving, involved hands from an intensive care unit are critical.

Patients who undergo organ transplants are routinely taken to the intensive care unit after surgery. There they are classified as being in critical but stable condition, even if the operation went well. The doctors and nurses keep a constant watch over them until they become strong enough to be transferred to a less intensive state of care.

New believers in Christ have undergone a serious organ transplant: they have received new hearts. They need careful follow-up and nurture if they are to make it. Leading people to new life in Christ is a cause for celebration. But we must remember they are in critical but stable condition.

PRAYER: Divine Nurturer, you continue to touch and nourish our life. Your mercy is tender. Your grace is amazing. Your patience and understanding is beyond our comprehension. Thank you for sustaining us and empowering us through your Spirit. As you nurture us by your unconditional love, let us nurture those you place in our lives.

As St. Francis of Assisi prayed, let us also:

Lord, make me an instrument of Thy peace. Where there is hatred let me sow love. Where there is injury pardon. Where there is doubt, faith. Where there is despair, hope. Where there is darkness, light. And where there is sadness, joy.

O Divine Master, let me not so much seek to be consoled as to console. To be understood as to understand. And to be loved as to love. For it is in giving that we receive. It is in pardoning that we are pardoned. And, it is in dying to self that we are raised to life eternal." Amen.

QUESTIONS AND REFLECTIONS

1. Locate a dictionary and look up the word "nurture". What is your definition of this word?

2. Give some examples of how you have received and given the ministry of nurture.

3. Nurture is essential to our physical and to our spiritual growth. List some of the similarities between physical and spiritual nurture.

4. Respond to this statement: The church should serve as an intensive care unit for wounded souls.

5. Do you agree that real nurture does not take place either long-distance nor vicariously?

6. What does the incarnation of God in Jesus Christ show us about "hands-on" nurture?

5

THE PLANTING—GETTING A GOOD START

"Just like a tree planted by the waters…I shall not be moved." Psalm 1:3

Getting off to a good start is essential. It's important to people and it's important to trees. Physicians and psychologists preach to us that the first five years in a human being's life are crucial in determining their physical and emotional health for the rest of their lives. So, too, botanists and horticulturists predict the health and longevity of plants and trees based upon their beginnings.

After their years of nurture in the nursery, and serving their time in the line-out beds for additional growth, fraser fir seedlings are transplanted to the fields. Here they will spend the next seven to eight years of their life, hopefully maturing into beautifully-shaped Christmas trees ready for harvesting.

Planting the fraser fir seedlings in the field involves using a tractor to pull a tobacco planter in tow. Two persons are seated on a dual-seater planter, depositing seedlings into the plowed rows. The seedlings are planted four feet apart so that there will be room for the trees to grow and mature over the next several years without crowding one another.

The Christmas tree farmer hopes that the first year will be positive for the young seedlings, as this first growing season often determines whether a tree will make it or not. This new beginning out in the field is a vulnerable time for the fraser fir seedling. Placement in this new environment and exposure to the various elements could lead to its demise. Yet, if the tiny seedling remained in the nursery, or line-out beds, it would never grow. It would never become what it was designed to be—a tree!

I heard a man share that he had once met a young man who dives for exotic fish for aquariums. He said one of the most popular aquarium fish is the shark. He explained that if you catch a small shark and confine it, it will stay a size proportionate to the aquarium. Sharks can be six inches long yet fully matured. But if you turn them loose in the ocean they grow to their normal length of eight feet.

Doesn't that happen sometimes in our Christian journey? Sometimes you see the cutest little six-inch Christians swimming around in a little pond. But if you put them into a larger arena—into the whole of creation—only then can they truly grow and mature for Christ's sake.

Just like the fish and just like the seedling, good health and positive growth come to us as we are well-grounded so that we may reach out. Stated another way, paradoxically, it is the established, healthy roots that enable us to use our God-given "wings" to fly. If we are not well-grounded in the truth and love of God, our attempts at "wing-time" will end in disappointment and even disaster.

But to those who seek and follow God's will and way, for them there is a secure grounding that enables a faith flight formation. In the words of a wise prophet: "They that wait upon the Lord (well-grounded) shall renew their strength; they shall mount up with wings as eagles (faith flight). They shall run and not be weary, they shall walk and not faint" (Isaiah 40:31).

When you are well-grounded (well-planted as a fraser fir seedling), and nurtured in love and trust you can then confidently reach out and risk loving others. This is the formula for growth in Christian discipleship: Stay well-grounded and planted in God's word, and out of this secure foundation take flight into a world that is filled with needs and hurts, and offer God's justice and righteousness and peace to all who will receive. As you practice and live this "rhythm of Christian discipleship" you will experience steady and exponential spiritual growth.

Let's learn a lesson of growth from the lobster. From time to time, lobster have to leave their shells in order to grow. They need the shell to protect them from being torn apart, yet when they grow, the old shell must be abandoned. If they did not abandon it, the old shell would soon become their prison—and finally their casket.

The tricky part for the lobster is the brief period of the time between when the old shell is discarded and the new one is formed. During that terribly vulnerable period, the transition must be scary to the lobster. Currents gleefully cartwheel them from coral to seaweed. Hungry schools of fish are ready to make them a part of their food chain. For awhile at least, that old shell must look pretty good.

We are not so different from lobsters. To change and grow, we must sometimes shed our shells—or come out of the nursery—we've depended upon. Discipleship means being so committed to Christ that when he bids us to follow, we will change, risk, grow, and leave our "shells" behind.

I recall walking around our very first field of fraser firs after their first year of growth. The planting had been a success. Generally you can figure about one thousand trees can be planted per cleared acre. On our three-acre plot almost all of the three-thousand trees looked green and healthy. Only a few had not survived the transplant out into the field. The first year had been a good one for these young seedlings and because of this their future looked very promising.

PRAYER: Lord, it is tempting to stay in the security of the nursery. There it is warm and safe and protective. Yet, if we stay there and never reach out to others we remain spiritual infants.

God, thank-you for the good grounding you provide us. It is a relationship of love and trust that never lets us go. And, it is out of this confidence that we are liberated to stretch and risk and grow. Not for the sake of selfish growth, but so that you and your kingdom may be blessed.

Help us to always remember our "first love"—to stay planted and grounded in your word so that we may reach out in love and compassion to your world. Through Christ we pray, Amen.

QUESTIONS AND REFLECTIONS

1. Whether planting in the proper soil or building on a good foundation, a good beginning is essential. What "good beginnings" in your life do you celebrate? What new beginnings might you need?

2. Interestingly, it is strong established "roots" in our life that enable us to employ our "wings" and fly. We require both roots and wings in order to live an abundant life. Discuss the "roots" in your life—those experiences, values, relationships, and beliefs that ground you. Then, discuss the "wings" in your life—those experiences of risking, reaching out, and going to new heights by faith.

3. "This is the formula for growth in Christian discipleship: stay well grounded and planted in God's Word, and out of this secure foundation take flight into a world that is filled with needs and hurts and offer God's justice, righteousness, and peace to all who will receive." Respond to this quote from chapter 5.

4. If everything were stripped away in your life what would be left standing? What is your foundation in life? What gives lasting meaning to you?

6

GOOD GROUND

"...the one who received the seed that fell on good soil is the man who hears the word and understands it. He produces a crop, yielding a hundred, sixty or thirty times what was sown"—Jesus (Matthew 13:23).

Before planting a crop of Christmas trees a wise grower takes soil samples of the area intended for planting. The condition of the ground is critical for optimal growth.

A good ground is a receptive ground. It is prepared to receive. It is ready to supply the proper nutrients for the seedlings.

Similarly, there is so much that our Heavenly Gardener wishes to show us and give us and do in and through us. Yet, often, we are not ready to receive. The "soil of our souls" is not prepared for what God has to sow in our life. Maybe we need to take a "soul sample", inviting God's Holy Spirit to take us underneath the surface, to the "root of the matter." The journey inward—to the soul issues—is always the most difficult. Yet, it also yields the only path to godly growth which yields joy and peace.

What messages are we hearing? From whom are we receiving guidance and direction for living? I have been accused at times on the domestic front (probably justifiably so) as having a condition known as "selective hearing". Selective hearing occurs when one practices the fine art of hearing what I wish to hear and tuning out the rest! For example, I may wish to hear the statement: "Supper is ready, come and eat." But, I may choose to filter out, "Would you please take out the garbage."

As we read and hear God's word where and when are we guilty of selective hearing? How often is our "soul soil" lacking in spiritual health and vitality due to missing God's message—through selective hearing, or not heeding what we have heard from the Lord? Sometimes in our waywardness we deliberately "march to our own drum" rather than God's cadence. What catches our attention? More importantly, what gets our obedience?

A Native American was in downtown New York, walking with his friend who lived in New York City. Suddenly he said, "I hear a cricket."

"Oh, you're crazy," his friend replied.

"No, I hear a cricket. I do! I'm sure of it."

"It's the noon hour. There are people bustling around, cars honking, taxis squeaking, noises from the city. I'm sure you can't hear it."

"I'm sure I do." He listened attentively and then walked around the corner, across the street, and looked all around. Finally on the corner he found a shrub in a large cement planter. He dug beneath the leaves and found a cricket. His friend was astounded. But the Cherokee said, "No. My ears are no different from yours. It simply depends on what you are listening to. Here, let me show you." He reached into his pocket and pulled out a handful of change—a few quarters, some dimes, nickels, and pennies. And he dropped it on the concrete. Every head in the area turned. "You see what I mean?' he said as he began picking up his coins. It all depends on what you are listening for."

Not only must we have "ears to hear" (Matthew 13:9), but we must learn what to listen for.

On one occasion, Jesus was seated by the Sea of Galilee. A large crowd of people gathered around him, so he got into a boat and sat there teaching them in parables as they stood on the shoreline. He said, "A farmer went out to sow his seed. As he was scattering the seed, some fell along the path, and the birds came and ate it up. Some fell on rocky places, where it did not have much soil. It sprang up quickly, because the soil was shallow. But when the sun came up, the plants were scorched, and they withered because they had no root. Other seed fell among thorns, which grew up and choked the plants. Still other seed fell on good soil, where it produced a crop—a hundred, sixty or thirty times what was sown. He who has ears, let him hear...Listen then to what the parable of the sower means: when anyone hears the message about the kingdom and does not understand it, the evil one comes and snatches away what was sown in his heart. This is the seed sown along the path. The one who received the seed that fell on rocky places is the man who hears the word and at once receives it with joy. But since he has no root, he lasts only a short time. When trouble or persecution comes because of the word, he quickly falls away. The one who received the seed that fell among the thorns is the man who hears the word, but the worries of this life and the deceitfulness of wealth choke it, making it unfruitful. But the one who received the seed that fell on good soil is the man who hears the word and understands it. He produces a crop, yielding a hundred, sixty or thirty times what was sown" (Matthew 13:3b-9; 18-23).

According to our Lord's words, the good soil represents the person who hears the word of God and assimilates it. Those who are open and receptive to God's word and working in their lives. Good ground, herein, equates to spiritual perception. Eyes and ears are open Godward. We look and listen for the word of God.

A former park ranger at Yellowstone National Park tells the story of a ranger leading a group of hikers to a fire lookout. The ranger was so intent on telling the hikers about the flowers and animals that he considered the messages on his two-way radio distracting, so he switched it off. Nearing the tower, the ranger was met by a nearly breathless lookout, who asked why he hadn't responded to the messages on his radio. A grizzly bear had been seen stalking the group, and the authorities were trying to warn them of the danger.

Whenever we tune out the messages God has sent us, we put at peril not only ourselves, but also those around us. Let us tune in to God's word so that we may avoid at all costs the condition expressed by the prophet Isaiah: "You will be ever hearing but never understanding; you will be ever seeing but never perceiving. For this people's heart has become calloused; they hardly hear with ears, and they have closed their eyes. Otherwise they might see with their eyes, hear with their ears, understand with their hearts and turn, and I would heal them" (Matthew 13:14b-17 as quoted by Jesus).

Let us keep our ears and eyes open and in tune with the things of God. This is the kind of life and fertile soil that will grow much fruit for the kingdom of God.

The collected soil samples from the Christmas tree fields, when tested, will inform the farmer of various soil contents such as acidity, phosphorous, potassium, and other elements. If the ph is low lime needs to be added to the land being tested. Phosphorous and nitrogen will be replenished in the soil as fertilizer is applied. Soil samples should be collected each year until the desired level is reached. Thereafter the grower might take soil samples every two to three years. This will help insure healthy soil. Good and healthy ground leads to healthy trees. Good and healthy "soul soil" leads to healthy growth in God's kingdom.

PRAYER: O God, we know your Word informs us "we reap what we sow." That is a painful truth because we have often sown unwisely. But you are the Master Gardener. And you have sowed seeds of grace and mercy and peace into our lives. We confess, Lord, some of that good seed has been wasted on us. Some has fallen on rocky ground in our soul. Other has found such shallow soil it cannot take root. Then, there are those times and seasons in our lives when we are so busy and distracted your will gets choked out of our days.

Help us, Lord to hear and heed your life-giving word. May our heart and mind and soul be good, fertile soil that is receptive to your sowing and abundant for your growing of fruit in your kingdom. Your kingdom come, your will be done on earth as it is in heaven. Amen.

QUESTIONS AND REFLECTIONS

1. In preparing the ground for the planting of Christmas trees the wise grower will first take soil samples to determine the status of the soil. In your life as a follower of Christ, what "soul soil" samples might you take to determine the receptivity in your life to God's word and will? Reflect upon some spiritual disciplines that are necessary in order for us to be open and receptive to God's word (Bible reading, prayer, holy communion, etc.).

2. In what ways and in what areas of your life might you be guilty of "selective hearing" with God?

3. In Matthew 13 Jesus speaks of at least four (4) soil types. Right now, is your "soul soil" more like:

    a. Good, healthy soil

    b. Hard, packed soil

    c. Rocky, sparse soil

    d. or, thorny, choked soil

7

A TALE OF TWO TRUETTS

"Do not be deceived: God cannot be mocked. A man reaps what he sows"
(Galatians 6:7 NIV).

The day was dawning beautifully in the mountains. It was perfect for some spring planting of seedlings. I was ready for a productive day in the field.

Several days before I had arranged with a grower of fraser fir seedlings (Tim) to meet him at Truett's home, where we could transfer the seedlings into my vehicle. Truett's place was about half way between Tim's home and my home so this seemed like a good plan. Tim had called Truett to ask his permission. Everything was panning out like clockwork.

It was early when I pulled into Truett's driveway. There was no sign of Tim yet, and no sign of anyone awake at Truett's place. So I sat in my car and waited. Fifteen minutes passed, then thirty. I became a little concerned.

So, I walked up to Truett's house and knocked on the door. It took several minutes and finally Truett opened the door, while wiping the sleep from his eyes. He looked out at me with surprise and asked, "How can I help you this morning?"

"Well, Truett, Tim R. t old me he called you so that I could pick up some Christmas tree seedlings at your place. I guess he's running late."

"Tell you what, let me get my boy out of bed and we'll go down to the seedling bed by the river and pull ya some of those nice seedlings. They oughta serve you well. Just pull your Jeep down that lower drive over there and we'll meet you."

So I jumped in my Jeep and drove down into the field by the river and waited. When they arrived, Truett, his boy, and I began pulling fraser fir seedlings out of the muddy soil. We must have pulled about a hundred seedlings when we heard a truck speeding down to our site with the driver blowing his horn. As the pickup got closer I could see it was Tim.

"Hey, Michael, I've been sittin' down at Truett's waitin' on you. Where you been?"

"I've been here at Truett's for over an hour. When you didn't show Truett decided to bring me down here to pull up some seedlings to take for planting."

That's when Tim informed me he had intended for us to meet at Truett C.'s and I had thought he meant Truett E.s. Both Truett s were in the Christmas tree business. And both Truett s were about halfway, but in different directions, between our two homes. But the fact that we had not communicated which Truett led us to different destinations.

Poor ole Truett E. must have been shocked when I showed up bright and early at his door with a request he hadn't even heard about. But, bless his soul, he didn't miss a beat. He and his son just marched right down to the bed of seedlings and began pulling trees, helping me feel as if no mistake had ever been made.

Tim and I had simply not communicated effectively. Sometimes what you do not say (omission) can be as dangerous and costly as what you do say.

A person can start out with the best of intentions but if you do not have the correct information and relay that information clearly, you can end up with the wrong results.

For example, a golden anniversary party was thrown for an elderly couple. The husband was moved by the occasion and wanted to tell his wife just how he felt about her. She was very hard of hearing, however, and often misunderstood what he had to say. With many family members and friends gathered around, he toasted her: "My dear wife, after fifty years I've found you tried and true!" Everyone smiled approval, but his wife said, "Eh?" He repeated in a louder voice, "After fifty years I've found you tried and true!" His wife was obviously angered and shot back, "Well, let me tell you something—after fifty years I'm tired of you, too!"

This elderly couple's interaction reminds us that poor communication can carry a large, and sometimes painful, price tag.

It is so often our human tendency to spontaneously speak before we actively listen. And, this unfair and discourteous practice seems to rear its head especially with those whom we are the closest. Good, active listening requires time and effort. It is not complicated, but it is hard work. How often do you, like myself, hear a person sharing something but the entire time you are focusing upon your own thoughts and cannot wait for them to finish speaking, and sometimes do not wait, but interrupt, so you can speak your mind?

Active listening is one of the ways by which we show another honor and respect. We care enough for them, even though we may radically disagree with them, that we carefully and thoughtfully listen to their words. There is required of us a slowing down—our thoughts and our being—and a single-pointed attention in order to practice the gift of active listening.

It is not that we always practice, or pretend to practice active listening skills, but if we are not willing to really listen to the other person we ought to have the courtesy and credibility to tell them.

For example, "I'm really sorry. I'm so emotionally drained. I'm afraid I can't really be a good listener right now. Let's talk later." Too often we go through the motions and pretensions of listening but we have not really discerned what has been said. Hearing is the ability to discriminate sound vibrations transmitted to the brain. Listening is making sense of what is heard.

Merely hearing without actively listening can lead not only to embarrassment but also to costly consequences. A striking example of the absence of active listening comes from the following military command. A colonel issued this directive to his executive officer.

"Tomorrow evening at approximately 2000 hours, Halley's Comet will be visible in this area, an event which occurs only once every 75 years. Have the men fall out in the battalion area in fatigues, and I will explain this rare phenomenon to them. In case of rain we will not be able to see anything, so assemble the men in the theatre and I will show them films of it."

Executive officer to company commander:

"By the order of the colonel, tomorrow at 2000 hours, Halley's Comet will appear above the battalion area. If it rains fall the men out in fatigues; then march to the theatre where the rare phenomenon will take place, something which occurs only every 75 years."

Company commander to lieutenant:

"By order of the colonel in fatigues at 2000 hours tomorrow evening, the phenomenal Halley's Comet will appear in the theater. In case of rain in the battalion area, the colonel will give another order, something which occurs once every 75 years."

Lieutenant to sergeant:

"Tomorrow at 2000 hours, the colonel, in fatigues, will appear in the theatre with Halley's Comet, something which happens every 75 years. If it rains, the colonel will order the comet into the battalion area."

Sergeant to squad:

"When it rains tomorrow at 2000 hours, the phenomenal 75-year-old General Halley, accompanied by the colonel, will drive his Comet through the battalion area theater in fatigues.

Mis-communication and garbled messages don't just occur in the military! It is so important to practice active listening skills in our every day interactions and relationships.

Some of the best instruction for good listening and communication located in the Bible is found in James chapter 1, verse 19: "My dear friends, you should be quick to listen and slow to speak or to get angry."

Someone has stated that this biblical emphasis upon "quick to listen" is reinforced by the fact that God created us with two ears and one mouth. We should listen twice as much as we speak.

The art and gift of listening—really listening—to another will go a long way in improving our relationships with our family, friends, and others. There are some simple, but effective steps we can take to be better listeners, and thereby improving our relationships.

A communication cycle (or loop) has three parts: message, feedback, and clarification. Often times within a counseling session I will have a couple practice this cycle. Person A shares a concern or issue for three minutes. Person B practices active listening, knowing that they will need to repeat back to Person A what they have just heard. By repeating back Person B is less apt to be preoccupied or to reactively prepare their own agenda. Rather, this forces Person B to listen carefully, putting aside their own reactions while trying to identify with the thoughts and feelings of Person A.

After 3 minutes of "A's" sharing, "B" will give a paraphrase without editorializing (i.e. attempting to get "B's" agenda thrown in), then Person A is asked to confirm or clarify their message. Person B is then invited to share for three minutes and the communication loop is completed (Message—Feedback—Clarification). This can be one of the best 10-minute segments we can ever invest in a relationship.

Ordinarily, we rush conversation. We make assumptions (as the above military example poignantly illustrates), jump to conclusions, and have our response ready before the other person even finishes speaking. Even though giving feedback may sound like an awkward and time consuming procedure, much more time and energy will be demanded when we do not take time for feedback.

In creative communication and active listening, feedback and clarification can become quick and useful ways to prevent or clear up needless misunderstandings. They are especially valuable when emotions are stirred. Hear again, and put into practice the instruction of James: "My dear friends, you should be quick to listen and slow to speak or to get angry."

Whenever I think of "A Tale of Two Truett s" I'm reminded how much we benefit from good, clear comunication. In the end it can spare us a lot of heartache.

PRAYER: O God, your communication is perfect! You desire to be in close relationship and communication with us, your people. Help us to spend more time listening to you and talking with you. May we not deceive one another; but, instead, may we be truthful and honest so we may believe one another.

And, yet, Lord, we confess that even our best falls short of your mark. Sometimes we forget. Sometimes even our carefully chosen words are misunderstood. Sometimes we leave unsaid what ought to be said and sometimes what we say would have been better left unspoken.

Help us to be clear and honest in our communication. Thank you for your grace and love that covers a multitude of sins. And help us to extend this same amazing grace to those who misunderstand us and to those we misunderstand. In the name of our compassionate Communicator we pray. Amen.

QUESTIONS AND REFLECTIONS

1. Positive communication involves both active listening and assertive sharing. How do you rate your active listening skills? How about your assertive (not aggressive) sharing skills?

2. Consider reading a book or an article or taking a workshop on positive communication skills.

3. In "A Tale of Two Truett s" crucial information was left out of the conversation, which led to wrong directions and incorrect destinations. How often do we withhold information (intended or unintended) and just assume that especially those closest to us know what we are talking about? How might this human tendency be lessened especially in your relationship with significant others?

8

ROOM TO GROW

"You obey the law of Christ when you offer each other a helping hand... We must each carry our own load" (Galatians 6:2,5).

When the tiny seedlings are in the nursery, and even in the field beds, they are in very close proximity to one another. But when they are transplanted to the fields they need room to grow. They require ample room for their root system to develop in the ground. They necessitate space for their branches to expand.

We found out the hard way with the first field of Christmas trees we planted. Normally fraser fir seedlings are planted about four feet apart. This way a tree growing 7 to 8 feet in height will have sufficient space to grow before it is harvested.

That first year we experimented by planting the seedlings three feet apart. Things went well until the fifth or sixth growing season. As the trees approached average Christmas tree size (seven feet or so) they became too crowded. There was not enough space between the trees to allow room for maintenance. Trees were "colliding" with one another, so we were forced to extract some trees in order to save their neighbors. We simply had not allowed enough room for the trees' maturation process.

There existed a delicate balance between planting as many trees as possible on an acre of land, and planting them close enough so they could more practically and efficiently be cared for; and, planting them sufficiently apart so there would be proper space to grow and be tended to.

This same need for togetherness and space exists in our inter-personal relationships. The extremes are damaging and painful to endure. At one extreme we can find ourselves estranged—cut off from one another. This involves too much space for too long a time. At the other extreme we can be enmeshed with another—smothered. Smothered can be just as damaging as cut off, for there is offered no space in which to stretch and grow.

Just as the Christmas trees wither and eventually die without the proper space for their roots to develop and their branches to spread and grow; so, too, for us as individuals we wither and die without an appropriate balance of connection (development of our roots) and space (development of our wings).

A few winters ago, heavy snows hit our state of North Carolina. Following a wet, six-inch snowfall, it was fascinating to see the effect along a local interstate highway.

Next to the highway stood several large groves of tall, young pine trees. The branches were bowed down with the heavy snow—so low that branches from one tree were often leaning against the trunk or branches of another.

Where trees stood alone, however, the effect of the heavy snow was different. The branches had become heavier, but without other trees to lean against, the branches snapped. They lay on the ground, dark and alone in the cold snow.

When the storms of life strike at us, we need to be standing close to those who love and care for us. The closer we stand, the more we will be able to hold up.

The secret to healthy and happy living seems to lie in that delicate balance of standing side by side and supporting one another, but having enough space in which to grow—affirming and asserting your own unique identity. Again, not being cut off in our relationships, but also not being smothered.

In St. Paul's epistle to the Galatians—chapter 6—he pens some instructions that remind us of this balance and rhythm of life—the "dance" of connectedness and separateness. Upon first reading, the two Pauline instructions seem diametrically opposed. Only a few phrases separate these seemingly contradictory teachings.

Yet, their complementarity seems to strike at the heart of our need for human interdependency. Paul writes, "You obey the law of Christ when you offer each other a helping hand." And then he says, "We must each carry our own load" (Galatians 6:3,5).

Well, which is it? Offer a helping hand or carry our own load? I do not perceive these statements as contradictory, but rather as complementary. There are times in a relationship when we reach out to "receive a helping hand"—times of brokenness and weakness that require some help. And there are other times when we "carry our own load", as we have the ability to do so. This is the rhythm of interdependency. This is the dance of give-and-take. This is about closeness and flexibility.

On November 20, 1988, the Los Angeles Times reported: "A screaming woman, trapped in a car dangling from a freeway transition road in East Los Angeles was rescued Saturday morning. The 19-year-old woman apparently fell asleep behind the wheel about 12:15 A.M. The car, which plunged through a guard rail was left dangling by its left rear wheel. A half dozen passing motorists stopped, grabbed some ropes from one of their vehicles, tied the ropes to the back of the woman's car, and hung on until the fire units arrived. A ladder was extended from below to help stabilize the car while firefighters tied the vehicle to tow trucks with cables and chains.

"Every time we would move the car," said one of the rescuers, "she'd yell and scream. She was in pain."

It took almost 21/2hours for the passers-by, CHP officers, tow truck drivers, and firefighters—about 25 people in all—to secure the car and pull the woman to safety.

"It was kinda funny," L.A. County Fire Capt. Ross Marshall recalled later. "She kept saying, "I'll do it myself.""

There are times when self-sufficiency goes too far!

On the other hand, there are dangers with being overly dependent upon others. People need breathing room. If we become too rigid, and too smothering, whether speaking of trees or humans, we sap the life right out of the subjects.

One marriage and family resource wisely states: "A rigid status quo orientation is indicative of pathology…Given the continuing shifts in age, family composition and the need for redefinition of rules in families, a family locked into a rigid equilibrium…is in trouble.—the most viable family systems are those where there is a more free-flowing balance…successful negotiation, positive and negative feedback…with few implicit rules and more explicit rules…" ("Family Process"; March 1979, pp. 12-13).

As concerns rigidity, I like what pastor Chuck Swindoll has to say (in the context of parenting), "Children are a lot like chickens…they need room to squawk, lay a few eggs, flap their wings, even fly the coop. Otherwise, let me warn you, all that lid-sitting will one day explode and you'll wish you had not taken such a protective stance…"

Finding the proper balance between dependency and independency; between closeness and flexibility, in our relationships is a constant process. It is dynamic, never static. Learning to live interdependently will lead to stability and flexibility in our relationships as it provides room to grow.

PRAYER: God of all people, you have created us to be in relationship—in relation with you and in relation with one another. You have made us to be interdependent with each other. Sometimes we need to provide a shoulder for someone to lean and cry upon, and sometimes we need to accept another's shoulder to lean and cry upon.

Give us the compassion to graciously come alongside when there is a legitimate need. Give us courage to assertively claim our unique identity and space. Help us to practice healthy boundary-setting. May we evidence the love that keeps us connected to others, and may we practice the discipline that insures we have time apart so that we have something of value to offer another. Beyond this, Lord, we thank you for your patient love that gives us room to grow. In the strong name of Jesus Christ we pray. Amen.

QUESTIONS AND REFLECTIONS

1. As you consider the significant others in your life, in what ways are you dependent upon these persons?

2. In what ways do you practice independence in these same relationships?

3. The goal for healthy relationships is to be neither too dependent upon others, nor too independent from others. Instead, to practice more interdependency. Consider some of your closest relationships. Do you find you are more dependent or independent with these persons?

4. Spend some time studying Galatians 6:2-5. In what ways does this passage promote or not promote interdependency?

5. Spend some time reflecting upon and studying your family of origin especially as regards levels of closeness and levels of flexibility. In what ways do you continue to practice these family "rules" in your relationships? In what ways have you changed from your family of origin patterns?

9

RECIPIENTS OF GOOD COUNSEL

Proverbs 15:22 "Plans fail for lack of counsel, but with many advisors they succeed."

When my partners and I first began Christmas tree farming we were "green". We were brand new…novices at this tree-growing enterprise.

Fortunately, one of my partners had a connection with a Christmas tree expert. It was a relative of his who for years had raised Christmas trees. This person rapidly became our main consultant.

We certainly made our share of "grower's errors"—especially during those first years—but I am convinced that the good and wise advice and counsel of this kind kinfolk enabled us to get off to a strong start.

We were not created to go this thing called life alone. We need one another's counsel, guidance, and support. There is no such thing as a self made man or woman! This is simply and truly a misnomer. We are the sum of our experiences, decisions, and relationships.

Alex Haley, the author of "Roots", has a picture in his office, showing a turtle sitting atop a fence. The picture is there to remind him of a lesson he learned long ago: "If you see a turtle on a fence post, you know he had some help."

Say's Alex, "Any time I start thinking, 'Wow, isn't this marvelous what I've done!' I look at that picture and remember how this turtle—me—got up on that post."

One of the surest ways to succeed at life—and any aspect of living—is to hear and heed the wise counsel of persons who "have been there and done that." We can avoid a lot of pitfalls and mistaken steps IF we will only listen to the voices of experience.

Solomon writes, "...in a multitude of counselors there is safety" (Proverbs 24:66). We are so prone to plunge ahead without first doing proper assessment, which includes hearing and considering the advice of others. We are so programmed in our Western world orientation to "fly solo" and ride "lone ranger" and act independently that we miss out on the necessary and healthy practice of surrounding ourselves with wise counselors.

We have a wise gentleman, John, in the congregation where I serve as pastor. If you were to tell him he is wise he would vehemently deny it. Interestingly, I have found those persons who possess great wisdom often seem to be those who do not claim to be wise. They are transparent. The wisdom of G od flows through them. They recognize they are not the source of this wisdom and insight.

And, so, before I make a major decision regarding our congregational life I want to run it past John first.

We all need some Johns and Jonis in our life...persons who help us gain proper perspective; persons who hold us accountable; persons who help us gain wisdom and understanding.

Do you know the difference between a wise person and a fool? The fool thinks he knows it all; the wise man knows he doesn't. The fool refuses guidance and instruction because he's got his own plan laid out in his mind and he doesn't want to be bothered with anyone else's ideas. The wise person knows that his plans are not perfect, so he is not ashamed to ask for advice.

Receiving counsel pays a lot of dividends. It loans us another lens through which to view a topic or dilemma. It keeps us from rushing headlong and prematurely into a decision. We may discover a totally new perspective on a problem we may be facing. And a wise counselor can help us appreciate and give thanks that we are not alone in the discernment process.

No one knows everything. No one person has all knowledge. But God has given each of us a little piece of the big picture. The more pieces we put together in advance of a decision, a choice, or an action, the greater our chances of success.

Billy Graham writes: "I heard about a young president of a company who instructed his secretary not to disturb him because he had an important appointment. The chairman of the board came in and said, "I want to see Mr. Jones." The secretary answered, "I'm terribly sorry, he cannot be disturbed; he has an important appointment."

The chairman became very angry. He banged open the door and saw the president of his cooperation on his knees in prayer. The chairman softly closed the door and asked the secretary, "Is this usual?" And she said, "Yes, he does that every morning." To which the chairman of the board responded, "No wonder I come to him for advice."

And so it was, Sam and Larry and I were blessed to have an experienced tree-grower come alongside us and provide us with good advice. His helpful counsel guided us to a successful start in the field.

PRAYER: Divine Counselor, impart to us your wisdom. Life is filled with so many overwhelming decisions and choices. Thank you for giving us your written word and your living Word to guide us. Thank you also for those wise and caring "counselors" you have placed in our life. Help us to hear and heed the advice of the godly. In Christ's name and for his sake we pray. Amen.

QUESTIONS AND REFLECTIONS

1. Recount some persons who have given you wise advice and counsel that made a positive difference in your life. What caused you to listen to these persons?

2. What in our human nature and Western culture reinforces "flying solo" and riding "lone ranger"?

3. Solomon writes: "...In a multitude of counselors there is safety" (Proverbs 24:6b). What is the wisdom of this proverb?

CULTIVATING

10

SHIN GUARDS AND SHEARING KNIVES

"There is a way that seems right to humankind, but the end is death."

In order to trim Christmas trees into that much-desired cone shape a hand-held shearer is used. The typical shearing knife has a sharp twelve-inch blade with a six-inch handle. Because the shearer is so extremely sharp, and therefore dangerous, a protective shin guard is strapped to the worker's leg(s). This protective guard has saved many-a-leg from being severely cut open.

One particular day I was out in the Christmas tree field shearing trees all alone—not a recommended practice. I had failed to bring my protective shin guard along. But, I reasoned, these trees need shearing and I'll be extra cautious.

Well, I had worked less than one hour when the slip-up occurred! I will never forget this accident as long as I live. The sharpened shearing knife hit my shin cutting through denim jeans and opening up my leg. I saw blood and I knew it was cut pretty bad. So, I wrapped one of my shirts around the injured area, found my keys, and drove to the hospital, about fifteen minutes away.

When I arrived at the hospital my brother, a physician, happened to be there. I informed him what had happened and he took me to an examining room and began, with the assistance of a nurse, treating my injury.

It was not only embarrassing to have done something so stupid; but, it was also a vulnerable feeling to lay on the examining table with my brother suturing my leg. I began to entertain thoughts such as: "I hope I was nice to my brother growing up." Or, "I sure hope he remembers me as being nice to him MOST of the time!"

Anyway, all went well as Kevin did a marvelous job of sewing up my leg after I had broken the cardinal commandments of shearing Christmas trees. Number one: Thou shalt never shear alone. And, number two: Thou shalt always wear your shin guard while shearing.

It is innate in us human beings to think we can get away with "breaking the law." We rationalize; we justify our rebel behavior; we convince ourselves that no ill consequences will befall us. Somehow we think that if we can do whatever we want to do we will experience real freedom. Yet, it never works that way. As we pursue our self-centered and selfish pursuits prison walls grow taller and tighter around us. Freedom does not mean the absence of constraints or moral absolutes.

Suppose, for example, a skydiver at 10,000 feet announces to the rest of the group, "I'm not using a parachute this time. I want freedom!"

The fact is that a skydiver is constrained by a greater law—the law of gravity. But when the skydiver chooses the "constraint" of the parachute, she is free to enjoy the exhilaration.

God's moral laws act in the same manner: they restrain, but they are absolutely necessary to enjoy the exhilaration of real freedom.

Real freedom requires disciplined restraint and wise choices. Sometimes our stubbornness and lack of discernment entraps us.

Consider and heed the lesson of the mallard. Early one morning Karen and I were awakened to a rattling sound coming from our living room. It sounded like something trying to find freedom from an enclosure. Upon inspecting we discovered a duck in our fireplace! It had come down the chimney and could not retreat that same way. The glass panels on the front of the fireplace prohibited (thankfully!) the bird's exit in that direction.

We contemplated how we might liberate this terrified and trapped fowl. We finally decided that as Karen opened the glass doors to the fireplace I would take a large blanket and grab the duck, which due to its fierce struggle was by now exhausted and subdued.

The doors were opened, the blanket was lifted, the bird was captured! We took the swaddled bird to the front porch of our home. And as I opened the blanket this beautiful mallard duck spread her wings and flew off into the majestic freedom for which she was created!

This "bird brain" did finally return to freedom, but only with outside intervention and protection. How often we fumble and stumble, going our own determined way, yet because of divine grace we are rescued and freed once again!

Thanks be to God for his commandments, boundaries, and messengers that keep us from destroying ourselves and others. And, thanks for God's amazing grace that saves us even in spite of ourselves and our foolish, sinful ways!

I am very grateful that my leg was not permanently damaged from my foolish mistake in the Christmas tree field. And, I am thankful my doctor brother was available to help me in my time of need. From that day forward I never sheared Christmas trees alone. I always made sure someone was on site; and, I always wore my shin protector. Guidelines and boundaries are truly for our own good.

PRAYER: Dear Heavenly Parent, thank you for the boundaries and commandments you give to us in your Word! We are a stubborn and rebellious people. I imagine you must really get impatient and frustrated with our determined and head-strong ways. Yet, you continue to offer yourself and your gracious guidance to us each day that we have life. Help us to see that your loving limits and compassionate commandments are just that—loving and compassionate! When we are obedient to your ways there is justice for all. May we see that indeed your law is given out of your grace. Because your love is limitless for humanity you placed limits upon us.

O Holy Shepherd, lead us in the paths of righteousness for your name's sake. May your rod and staff guide and comfort us. Amen.

QUESTIONS AND REFLECTIONS

1. God places guards and guides in our lives. List some of these with gratitude.

2. What are some ways you have observed God using you and protecting you "in spite of yourself"?

3. The 23rd Psalm assures the believer: "Even though I walk through the valley of the shadow of death, I will fear no evil, for Thou art with me. Thy rod and Thy staff they comfort me." Explain and discuss how the "rod" and the "staff" provide comfort.

4. The Ten Commandments are not the "Ten Suggestions". They are given by divinity to humanity for our protection and for our liberation. Review these ten life-giving statements and guidelines and consider how each of them is for the good of ourselves and humanity (Exodus 20:1-17).

11

PRUNING THE PINES

"He cuts off every branch in me that bears no fruit, while every branch that does bear fruit he prunes so that it will be even more fruitful" (John 15:2 NIV).

As Christmas trees mature in the field they must be sheared in order to create that much-desired pyramid shape. A shearing knife is held at an angle around each side of the tree, extracting protruding and non-conformist branches that detract from the coveted Christmas tree contours. The shearing process is long in time and laborious in energy. But the results make all the difference.

There is an art to pruning. The pruner is required to have an experienced eye—a vision that is trained to spatial symmetry. This craftsman knows how to bring the proper order and design out of "rebellious branches." The artist is required to have a desired image and result in mind so that the Christmas tree-shape may be created.

I knew of a wood-carver in the North Carolina mountains who carved wooden dogs. People came from far away to purchase these beautifully crafted creatures. On one occasion the mountaineer wood-crafter was asked, "How do you make these dogs?" He replied, "Oh, it ain't too hard. I jus' take a block of wood and carve away anything that don't look like a dog."

The crafting of critters and the pruning of pines reminds me that God desires to shape our lives—to shape our lives more and more into the image of Jesus Christ. When we submit ourselves to this providential pruning process God can shape us and use us in powerful ways!

The pruning process is never easy. And, it is never painless. It hurts to be pruned because some excising is taking place. God's spiritual surgery is never easy, but it is always fruitful.

As the pruner shears the tree s and the potter shapes the clay, so too we must allow God to design our lives after his divine will. In the words of a familiar hymn:

> "Have thine own way, Lord!
> Have thine own way!
> Thou are the potter, I am the clay.
> Mold me and make me after thy will
> While I am waiting, yielded and still."

In the 15th chapter of John's Gospel Jesus teaches spiritual "pruning truths" through an object lesson. He speaks of a grapevine. Jesus is the true vine. God is the gardener who tends the vine. The followers of Christ are the branches. We must stay joined to the true vine (Jesus) if we wish to experience and share abundant life. The word Jesus uses for this staying joined is "abide." In fact, the concept of abiding in Jesus is so crucial that Jesus used the term "abide" ten times in eleven verses.

What does "abiding in Jesus Christ" mean? It means life. It means living with Christ daily. It means an intimate relationship—living in Christ and Christ living in you.

The real, authentic Vine has life-producing powers flowing through it. The Vine supplies the branches with the good, nourishing food that leads to healthy growth.

While Christ is the Vine, God is the divine Gardener. And, like any good, caring gardener, he breaks off branches that are dead and in the way of new growth. And, he prunes every branch that does not bear sufficient fruit, so that it will be clean and bear more fruit. The gardener removes the branches that are bearing no fruit, and he prunes those that are not bearing enough fruit.

Merrill Tenny writes:

"Viticulture…consists mainly of pruning. In pruning a vine, two principles are generally observed: first, all dead wood must be ruthlessly removed; and second, the live wood must be cut back drastically. Dead wood harbors insects and disease and may cause the vine to rot, to say nothing of being unproductive and unsightly. Live wood must be trimmed back in order to prevent such heavy growth that the life of the vine goes into the wood rather than into fruit. The vineyards in the early spring look like a collection of barren, bleeding stumps; but in the fall they are filled with luxuriant purple grapes. As the farmer wields the pruning knife in his vines, so God cuts dead wood out from among his saints and often cuts back the living wood so far that his method seems cruel. Nevertheless, from those who have suffered the most there often comes the greatest fruitfulness."

The Christmas tree farmer must trim the tree so that the unwieldy branches conform to the proper size and shape. What "pruning" does the divine Gardener need to perform in your life? What "dead wood" needs to be removed? What areas need some "tree trimming" so that more fruit, and a more Christmas tree like shape, might be produced?

God, the Master Gardener has placed a beautiful potential in each and every human soul. If we will submit to his shaping, pruning, and carving we will be pleasantly astonished at the outcome in our lives.

This shaping process is described in a poem from "The Way of Chuang Tzu".

The Woodcarver

Khing, the master carver made a bell stand
Of precious wood. When it was finished,
All who saw it were astounded. They said it must be
The work of spirits.
The Prince of Lu said to the master carver:
"What is your secret?"

Khing replied, "I am only a workman:
I have no secret. There is only this:
When I began to think about the work you commanded
I guarded my spirit, did not expend it
On trifles, that were not to the point.
I fasted in order to set
My heart at rest.
After three days fasting, I had forgotten gain and success.
After five days
I had forgotten my body
With all its limbs.
"By this time all thought of your Highness
And of the court had faded away.
All that might distract me from the work
Had vanished.
I was collected in the single thought
Of the bell stand.
"Then I went to the forest
To see the trees in their own natural state.
When the right tree appeared before my eyes,
The bell stand also appeared in it, clearly, beyond doubt.
All I had to do was to put forth my hand
And begin.

If I had not met this particular tree
There would have been
No bell stand at all.
"What happened"
My own thought
Encountered the hidden potential in the wood;
From this live encounter came the work
Which you ascribe to the spirits."

PRAYER: O Divine Gardener, thank you for seeing the beautiful and wonderful potential in each one of us. We are created by you in your likeness! As the woodcarver looks at the tree and sees a bell-table, so you, the Divine Gardener, look at our lives and see a treasured masterpiece.

Help us, Lord, to see with your eyes. Enable us to see the power and the love of God that is within us. There is a "song of God" within each of us. How tragic to die with the song never sung...never shared...never expressed!

Some of us, O God, do not sense this marvelous image-of-God potential within us. Help us to open our lives to your gracious gifts of mercy, grace, and peace so that we may believe, receive, and be shaped more and more into the likeness of your Son, our Lord and Savior, Jesus Christ. Amen.

QUESTIONS AND REFLECTIONS

1. The mountain wood-carver stated: "I jus' take a block of wood and carve away anything that don't look like a dog." How does this have application to our life in God's the master Craftsman's hands?

2. The two main actions of the pruner are to cut out the old, dead vines; and, to cut way back the healthy vines. Why are both these actions necessary for a healthy vine? And, how do these pruning principles apply to our spiritual life?

3. What "dead wood" needs to be removed from your life?

4. What pruning of healthy aspects of your faith walk needs to happen for you to be a stronger, more vital Christian disciple?

12

TWO TOPS

"You cannot be the slave of two masters! You will like one more than the other or be more loyal to one than the other" (Matthew 6:24).

There are two cardinal rules when it comes to topping a Christmas tree. First, you must clip the top leader so that it does not become too long proportionate to the trees size, thus resulting in a disproportionate tree.

Second, you must make certain there is a designated top leader so that the tree does not develop two or more tops. This mandates choosing which of the multiple tops is best to keep, and cutting off the other leader branches.

Many times while walking through the Christmas tree fields, I have studied and struggled over which top to keep and which to extract. After careful examination you cut off a top and hope that the best decision was made. The words of a Robert Frost poem come to mind as I consider this choosing process: "Two roads diverged in a yellow wood and sorry I could not travel both; and being one traveler, long I stood and looked down one as long as I could to where they met in the underbrush. I took the road less traveled and it has made all the difference."

As God's people we wish to make the best choices in life. For, the choices we make affect others and they affect the rest of our lives. We do need to give great care to our decisions and choices…choices which possess the potential and power to shape our character and shape our lives. This is about making the wisest decisions and best choices reliant upon God's gift of discernment. This "best" way will not often be the easiest way. It will frequently not be the natural way for us. Yet, if it is God's way it will yield good growth for our lives.

When the strongest, straightest, and most strategically-located top is selected for the tree, the result will be a much-desired, beautiful Christmas tree. When the grower takes the time and effort to select the best top possible the dividends are well worth this effort at harvest time.

Very often good "choice-making" involves deferred-gratification. The grower clips off a leader branch, for example, so that years later the tree is better proportioned and much more symmetrical in shape.

So, too, our lives need a spiritual focus that practices a long obedience in the same direction. Tiny seeds, planted today and nurtured become the strong developed plants of tomorrow. Small seedlings placed in the ground and cared for, grow into the mature Christmas trees several years later.

Reaching growth goals requires staying focused. Single-pointed attention is the secret to both making the most of the present moment and obtaining the goal of the future.

Listen to the "focus" language and single-pointed attention, as St. Paul expresses his mission statement: "Not that I have already obtained this (resurrection from the dead) or have already reached the goal; but I press on to make it my own, because Christ Jesus has made me his own. Beloved, I do not consider that I have made it my own, but this one thing I do: forgetting what lies behind, and straining forward to what lies ahead. I press on toward the goal for the prize of the heavenly call of God in Christ Jesus..." (Philippians 3:12-14).

"ONE thing I do," says Paul, "straining forward...pressing on toward the goal...focusing upon the call of God in Christ Jesus..." There are many distractions. Short-cuts are tempting. Other paths appear more rewarding for the moment. Yet, only those who stay focused, with single-pointed attention to the will and way of Christ Jesus will receive the prize.

The Christian committed to the discipleship call of Christ will consider everything secondary that does not conform to the will of God. One cannot be a disciple of Christ and a disciple of anyone (including self) or anything else. Jesus asks to be Lord (Director) of our life.

In his Sermon on the Mountain, Jesus speaks of this exclusive Lordship: "You cannot be the slave of two masters! You will like one more than the other or be more loyal to one than the other..." (Matthew 6:24).

I call this seeking to serve two or more masters "spiritual schizophrenia." It dichotomizes our life and scatters our attention to the point of spiritual suicide! Our allegiance is called for in so many directions that we are pulled apart.

The remedy to this spiritual schizophrenia is to practice single-pointed attention and get rid of those attitudes and behaviors that do not conform to God's will.

The writer of Hebrews, describing the Christian journey as a road race, instructs us with these words: "We must get rid of everything that slows us down." Anything that gets us off track must be discarded. All the negative baggage, harmful distractions—which sometimes are not bad in and of themselves, but they are simply not the best—sinful thoughts and actions must go!

Sometimes it doesn't take much to slow us down in our "race". In fact, it's often the "small" things in life that begin to loom large.

Did you know that scientists are now telling us that a series of slits, not a giant gash, sank the Titanic? The opulent, 900-foot cruise ship in 1912 was on its maiden voyage, from England to New York. Fifteen hundred people died in the worst maritime disaster of all time.

The most widely held theory is that the ship hit an iceberg, which opened a huge gash in the side of the liner. But an international team of divers and scientists recently used sound waves to probe through the wreckage, buried in mud two-and-a-half miles deep. Their discovery? The damage was surprisingly small. Instead of the huge gash, they found six relatively narrow slits across the six watertight holds.

"Everything that could go wrong did," said William Garzke, Jr., a naval architect who helped the team with their analysis.

Small damage, below the waterline and invisible to most can sink a huge ship. In the same way, small compromises and negative choices can ultimately sink a person's character and reputation.

Right-now choices have long-term effects. Even small decisions we make today have the power to shape all our tomorrows.

Ronald Meredith describes one quiet night in early spring:

"Suddenly out of the night came the sound of wild geese flying. I ran to the house and breathlessly announced the excitement I felt. What is to compare with wild geese across the moon?

It might have ended there except for the sight of our tame mallards on the pond. They heard the wild call they had once known. The honking out of the night sent little arrows of prompting deep into their wild yesterdays. Their wings, fluttered a feeble response. The urge to fly—to take their place in the sky for which God made them—was sounding in their feathered breasts, but they never raised from the water.

The matter had been settled long ago. The corn of the barnyard was too tempting! Now their desire to fly only made them uncomfortable.

Cutting a few inches off a single branch of a young pine may seem an insignificant matter. Yet, this pruning selection can make all the difference in years to come—as to whether the tree will grow into a beautifully-shaped Christmas tree or a mis-shapened reject.

So, too, in our lives the small, seemingly incidental choices we make daily hold the enormous capacity to shape us into Christ-like followers, or to lead us down a self-centered defeatist road. A gracious God calls us, and permits us, to choose!

PRAYER: O God, the choices before us loom large!...and complicated! Sometimes we want to do your will but we truly don't know your will. Other times, we know your will but, to be very honest, it's the last thing we want to do!

Lord, choices have shaped our life. Some for good. Some not so good. Yet, by your grace and mercy you have sustained us and kept us from falling!

There is a God-shaped vacuum that you have created deep in our souls. We cannot know peace until our choices bring us into harmony with your divine will.

As much as we resist you...thank you for not creating us as puppets on a string. You have created us with the capacity to choose. And you honor us with the liberty of free will.

May we exercise this liberty to do your will on earth as it is in heaven and thereby discover purpose and peace for our days. In Jesus' name, Amen.

QUESTIONS AND REFLECTIONS

1. Much of wise decision making involves deferred gratification—to put off some immediate want in pursuit of a worthy future goal. Legend NFL Coach Tom Landry once shared that his job was to take a group of grown men and make them do what they least wanted to do (work hard on conditioning and football fundamentals) day after day so that they could obtain what they most desired (a super bowl championship).

   In an age of immediate gratification, what are some specific actions we can take in order to make wise decisions and choices for the future?

2. Sometimes we get pulled in so many directions! And many of the "pullings" are not bad things in and of themselves. Yet, we must keep our focus. We must stay centered on Jesus Christ for our life to find proper balance.

   Someone has said "the main thing is to keep the main thing the main thing". What are some spiritual disciplines and habits that will help us with single-pointed attention upon Christ?

3. The writer of the book of Hebrews challenges us to "get rid of everything that slows us down." What might God be calling you to rid of so that you can more effectively and faithfully run the Christian race?

4. As with the great ship the Titantic, sometimes small, almost insignificant damage, below the waterline, can have huge consequences. What can we do to avoid even these so-called "small" damages in life?.

13

BEES IN THE TREES

"Be self-controlled and alert. Your enemy the devil prowls around like a roaring lion looking for someone to devour" (I Peter 5:8).

Everything pointed to a wonderful and beautiful day. The autumn sun beamed brightly out of the cloudless sky. Sam, Larry, and I were in the Christmas tree field, excited over the prospect of accomplishing much before sundown.

I was basking in the warmth of the morning sunshine, while carefully and methodically trimming the trees. Then it happened. My sharp shearing knife made contact with, and sliced in half, a hidden hornets nest!

The sharp stings of these angry insects yielded new meaning to the phrase "as mad as a hornet"! Mad, indeed, as they chased me up one row of trees, and over into another. Of all days for me to be wearing my old blue jeans with large holes in both knees! In addition to stinging me on the hands and face, these homeless hornets entered at the knees and stung up and down my thighs. The pain was immense and I found myself yelling and leaping and slapping to rid myself of this unwanted company!

After awhile I re-gained my composure and lay in the field resting from the enormous expenditure of adrenalin and energy. Sam and Larry, observing that I was finally okay, expressed that they'd "never seen a Methodist preacher dance like that before"! And, furthermore, they'd never heard a preacher, not even a charismatic one, jump and shout like I had through those rows of pines!

What started out as an absolutely picture-perfect, everything-going-fine day, was interrupted by danger hidden in a tree.

Many words in the Bible warn us and remind us to be alert. Watch. Don't be lulled to sleep. Stay awake.

I Peter 5:8 exhorts us to "Be on guard, and stay awake. Your enemy the devil, is like a roaring lion, sneaking around to find someone to attack."

When life is on "cruise control" it can lead to complacency. To the eye, the tree seems like a safe target upon which the shearing knife may land; but, take warning, watch out there may be bees in the trees!

And all of a sudden your day, and your world, changes.

Steve Green, who sang six years with Bill and Gloria Gaither, tells about getting to know some of the work crews in the large auditoriums where their concerts were held.

The Gaithers prefer concerts-in-the-round, which means extra work for the "riggers", who walk the four-inch rafter beams—often a hundred feet above the concrete floor—to hang sound speakers and spotlights. For such work, understandably, they are very well paid.

"The fellows I talked to weren't bothered by the sight of looking down a hundred feet," says Green. "What they didn't like, they said, were jobs in buildings that had false ceilings—accoustical tile slung just a couple of feet below the rafters. They were still high in the air, and if they slipped, their weight would smash right through the flimsy tile. But their minds seemed to play tricks on them, lulling them into carelessness."

Satan's business is not so much in scaring us to death as persuading us that the danger of a spiritual fall is minimal. No wonder Peter advised us to "Resist the Devil, standing firm in the faith."

Be vigilant. Beware when life appears to be on cruise. Attend to the details. Stay focused on Christ. Meditate and concentrate on the true, the pure, the right and the good. Do not permit your mind to wander off course. Keep your eyes on the goal.

On March 6, 1987, Eamon Coughlan, the Irish world record holder at 1500 meters, was running in a qualifying heat at the World Indoor Track Championships in Indianapolis. With two and a half laps left, he was tripped. He fell, but he got up and with great effort managed to catch the leaders. With only twenty yards left in the r ace, he was in third place—good enough to qualify for the finals.

He looked over his shoulder to the inside, and, seeing no one, he let up. But another runner, charging hard on the outside, passed Coughlan a yard before the finish, thus eliminating him from the finals. Coughlan's great comeback effort was rendered worthless by taking his eyes off the finish line.

It's tempting to let up when the sights around us look favorable. It's very easy to lose focus and grow negative in our thinking and in our actions. But we finish well in the Christian race only when we fix our eyes on the goal: Jesus Christ our Master and Redeemer.

One careless cut with the shearing knife into the trees can remind us of the need to "Bee Vigilant" in life.

PRAYER: God, who never sleeps nor slumbers, we are quick to forget and neglect. Our minds wander and our attention span is short term, at best. In our wandering guide us back to your way. Help us keep our focus upon you, O Lord, for that which clamors for and so often captivates our attention is frequently temporal and disillusioning. But our soul is at rest when our minds are staid upon you. Amen.

QUESTIONS AND REFLECTIONS

1. Read I Peter 5:8-11. According to this scripture, how are we as Christians to stand firm and be alert?

2. Sometimes the "sunny, bright days" and "smooth sailing" can put us on cruise control or automatic pilot in life. What are the possible dangers with this posture?

3. Respond to this statement: "Satan's business is not so much in scaring us to death as in persuading us that the danger of a spiritual fall is minimal."

14

A DRY SEASON

"Every tree in the forest will know that I, the Lord, can bring down tall trees and help short ones grow. I dry up green trees and make dry ones green. I, the Lord, have spoken, and I will keep my word" (Ezekiel 17:24).

It had been a dry, disastrous season for growing! The seedlings that had been planted that spring had a high casualty rate. Even the mature trees with a more developed root system were stressed. The green on their needles was not as bright. Many branches were losing their needles to the drought. As the rain deficit continued to grow the trees continued taking a toll.

We experience "dry" times in our life that also take their toll upon us. Losses can bring on these dry times. Life changes so quickly and we find ourselves in the "desert of despair"—wandering aimlessly, attempting to find help and hope amidst our grief and loss.

Writer Edgar Jackson graphically describes this groping grief:

-Grief is a young widow trying to raise her three children alone.

-Grief is the man so filled with shocked uncertainty and confusion that he strikes out at the nearest person.

-Grief is a mother walking to a nearby cemetery to stand quietly and alone a few moments before going about the tasks of the day. She knows that a part of her is in the cemetery just as part of her is in her daily work.

-Grief is the silent, knife-like terror and sadness that comes a hundred times a day, when you start to speak to someone who is no longer there.

-Grief is the emptiness that comes when you eat alone after eating with another for many years.

-Grief is teaching yourself to go to bed without saying good night to the one who has died.

-Grief is the helpless wishing that things were different when you know they are not and never will be again.

-Grief is a whole cluster of adjustments, apprehensions, and uncertainties that strike life in its forward progress and make it difficult to redirect the energies of life.

Undoubtedly, the season of grief—a time of drought—when emotional resources seem depleted—is difficult to navigate and even sometimes near impossible to tolerate.

Yet, as the Psalmist affirms, we are not alone in the "valley of drought": "Even though I walk through the valley of death you are with me, O Lord, your rod and your staff comfort me…" In fact, the writer of the 23rd Psalm joyfully testifies: "The Lord is my shepherd I shall not want. He makes me lie down in green pastures. He leads me beside still waters. He restores my soul. He leads me in paths of righteousness for his name's sake…"

In the midst of our driest season. In the grip of our greatest grief our faith instructs us that the Lord will meet us there and never leave us alone—"Even though I walk through the valley of death, you, O Lord, are with me…"

In fact, grief is a good gift from God. The "dry", wilderness experiences of life can be an important and life-giving time of introspection and examination. We can learn and/or re-learn our need of Divinity for our days. The dry times can help facilitate the green, growing times. The barren winter season has its own unique beauty and necessity. If there were no winter season would we truly appreciate the spring? Sometimes our fields must lie fallow. Sometimes there is need of stopping and taking inventory before the new growth appears. The work of good grief can provide this necessary reflection and re-direction.

One of the driest years in recorded history forced many of us Christmas tree farmers to replace the brown, dead trees with green, living seedlings. Thankfully the drought ended and the rains returned and the trees began once more to grow and flourish.

O Holy Comforter, some seasons in our life are filled with pain, loss, and grief. We know neither where to turn or what to do in the midst of our lonely despair. Help us to hold fast to your almighty and all-loving hands and to be re-assured that you will never leave nor forsake us. Keep us from fear of the dry times but rather to faithfully face the wilderness knowing that you, O Lord, will be with us through the most difficult days. As we know your presence in the grief may we experience, along with the Psalmist, the "still waters" and the "green pastures" that lead to a deeper and closer walk with you our Good Shepherd, in whose name we pray, Amen.

QUESTIONS AND REFLECTIONS

1. Recall some of the "dry", desert times in your life. During those tough times, what were some of your thoughts and feelings?

2. Although we would probably never seek those dry times in our spiritual journey, they come to all of us at some time or another. How can "dry" times be viewed as positive times? For example, in what ways is grief a gift from God?

3. Respond to this statement: "Sometimes our fields must lie fallow. Sometimes there is need of stopping and taking inventory before the new growth appears."

15

EACH ONE IS UNIQUE

"The tree which moves some to tears of joy is in the eyes of others only a green thing that stands in the way."—William Blake

One of my favorite things to do is walk through the rows and rows of Christmas trees admiring their beauty and variety. No two trees are the same! Even though planted side-by-side during the same year, and from the same nursery, each tree is unique. The trees come in different heights, different widths, and a variety of shades of green. Some are very full with branches, others have a dearth of limbs.

Yet each tree has its own unique, special beauty and style. During the holiday season persons would arrive at our Christmas tree farm to choose and cut their own tree. Often, the trees the guests chose would not be the ones I would have chosen. But, then, I kept those thoughts to myself. Because beauty is in the eye of the beholder. Every tree is beautiful and wonderful to someone.

Some even have an affinity for a bare and straggly "Charlie Brown" type Christmas tree. A tree that would never be a "hit" in many people's eyes.

Probably no composer has captured the musical heart and soul of America as did Irving Berlin. In addition to familiar favorites such as "God Bless America" and "Easter Parade," he wrote, "I'm Dreaming of a White Christmas," which still ranks as the all-time best-selling musical score.

In an interview with the San Diego Union, Don Freeman asked Berlin, "Is there any question you've never been asked that you would like someone to ask you?"

"Well, yes, there is one," he replied. "What do you think of the many songs you've written that didn't become hits?" My reply would be that I still think they are wonderful."

God, too, has a permanent pride in what—and whom—he has made. He thinks each of his children is wonderful. Whether they are a "hit" in the eyes of others or not he will always think they are wonderful!

Whether a "Charlie Brown" Christmas tree or a large, full evergreen, each tree seems to find its way into someone's home for the holidays. Each tree lends a unique style and beauty. This uniqueness principle is true whether speaking of Christmas trees, snow flakes, or human beings. Every person is a unique reflection of God's divine image. Of the billions of people in the world no two set of finger prints are the same, and no two temperaments or personalities are alike!

The rich diversity of humanity has been designed by divinity! What a myriad of colors and convictions and personalities we are! We should give our Creator thanks for this wonderful multitude of differences. Because uniqueness makes completeness. No one person, or group, holds a monopoly on what is truth and what is right. Life is too big and too complex for any person or group or denomination to claim they possess the only right way.

Instead, in genuine humility we should hold fast to our convictions while being open-minded to others who do not share the same opinions and convictions. We should always remember that we may be myopic on an issue and we therefore can potentially learn from others.

I love the account told of Methodist evangelist E. Stanley Jones, who was leading one of his spiritual retreats. At one point on this retreat Jones invited the participants to take out a sheet of paper and a pencil and write down some sins with which each person was struggling. A fellow in the crowd blurted out: "Dr. Jones, what if you don't have anything to write down?' To which Stanley Jones quickly and wisely replied: "Write down: 'I have nothing to write down!' Because if you don't have anything to write down then that is your problem."

If we feel we have no problems, that there is no sin in our lives, then that, for certain, is our problem. The Bible poignantly reminds us: "For all have sinned and come short of the glory of God."

Yet, as we confess our sins before God and others we find forgiveness and grace abounding. And, we discover our relationship with our "neighbor" improved for we are no longer in a condescending, self-righteous posture…which in turn allows us to see the unique beauty in another person's life and convictions.

Far too frequently we develop a negative competition with our sisters and brothers in the Christian faith, instead of celebrating a complementarity. Negative competition is based upon someone winning and another losing. Complementarity, however, is based upon a win-win outcome. Complementarity does not mean you don't play the game and play your very best. Rather, as you play your very best you value the validity, and respect the rights, of that other person.

Allow me to illustrate from the National Football League:

Gene Stallings tells of an incident when he was defensive backfield coach of the Dallas Cowboys. Two All-Pro players, Charlie Waters and Cliff Harris, were sitting in front of their lockers after playing a tough game against the Washington Redskins. They were still in their uniforms, and their heads were bowed in exhaustion. Waters said to Harris, "By the way Cliff, what was the final score?"

As shown by these great players, excellence isn't determined by comparing our score to someone else's. Excellence comes from giving your very best, no matter what the score. In this way, with this attitude that embraces complementarity, you can appreciate the effort and talents of the other, while at the same time affirming your own efforts and talents.

This "complementary" way I believe to be the way of our Savior and Lord Jesus Christ, who listened and cared deeply for all persons, yet he would not compromise upon his Heavenly Father's will. At the same time he respected and permitted the personal choice and free will of others. He did not manipulate nor coerce. Instead, he told the truth in love. Then persons could make their own choices. This gracious posture is strikingly and intimately observed at Golgotha, while Jesus is hanging on a Roman cross between two criminals.

The one criminal confesses his sin to Christ ("Then he said, 'Jesus, remember me when you come into your kingdom.'" Luke 23:42) while the other rejects Jesus ("One of the criminals who hung there hurled insults at him: 'Aren't you the Christ? Save yourself and us!'" Luke 23:40).

Someone has stated that from a human perspective Jesus batted only .500 from the cross, while dying for the world. Yet, Jesus cares so deeply for us that he allows us to make our own decisions and choices. Imagine! A God who loves us so much he respects and honors us enough to permit us to make our own unique choices, even while stretched out on a tree for us!

Though we may differ radically and vehemently with another we should respect their right to make a decision different from ours. This respectful attitude leads to a philosophy that should be practiced and embraced in all relationships and communities: Agree to disagree agreeably.

In order to truly appreciate another's position and/or viewpoint we must be secure in our own position and perspective. To authentically affirm a differing opinion from our own necessitates an affirmation of our own opinion as well.

This is one of the great mysteries which lead to a tranquil and meaningful life. The Great Commandment taken from the Bible exhorts us to, "Love the Lord your God with all your heart and mind and soul and your neighbor as yourself."

It is striking that love for God, love for neighbor, and love for self can not be separated! In order to love our self we must first know and experience God's love and love God. In order to love our neighbor we must first love our self. If we are to hold our neighbor in high esteem we must possess a positive self-esteem. In order to appreciate and affirm unique beauty in a fellow human being we must appreciate and affirm the unique beauty in our own character.

Mezzo-soprano Susan Graham is one of opera's rising young stars. In a profile for a publisher, Graham was asked to compare her voice with that of one of opera's legendary mezzo-sopranos, Cecilia Bartoli—would Susan be the next Bartoli?

Graham asserted, "I'm not sure I want to be the next anyone. I'd rather be the first Susan Graham."

What a great response! For Ms Graham it was not about comparison and negative competition. Rather, it was about God-ordained variety and complementarity uniqueness. Susan Graham appreciated Cecilia Bartoli's great voice and she affirmed her own abilities.

Graham exemplified the healthy "detachment—attachment" principle of relationships. We must "detach" from another before we can truly "attach." That is, we must develop a strong, secure sense of our self before we have a self to offer to another. If our identity and sense of worth and value derives from enmeshment in another's life and world, then we present only a pseudo-self that feeds like a dependent parasite upon another's life being unable to stand on our own two feet.

In contrast, when we affirm our God-given uniqueness and specialness, and when we are able to celebrate our contributions, as well as the contributions of others, then we are able to authentically attach in healthy relationships with others—relationships where there exists mutual respect, gracious acceptance of differences, and a rhythm of give-and-take (interdependency).

As I meander through the long green rows of trees, I stop and admire the unique beauty of each particular tree. Most days all I see is a large field of Christmas trees where all the greens and the branches seem to merge together in a "sea of trees." But not today. This time I look more closely at the distinct individual beauty of each tree. I take time to examine the individual branches and to carefully consider the contour of the trees.

Amazingly, no two trees are alike! And if you look closely and carefully you will see a unique beauty in each tree.

PRAYER: Heavenly Parent of all humanity, you made us each one in your image. Yet within that human reflection of divinity there is a richness of diversity and variety. There is female and male, variety of skin color, and multiplicity of cultures and personalities—all in their uniqueness helping to bring clarity and complementarity to your heavenly image.

O God, we are so quick to judge others on appearances and first encounters without really knowing them. Like beholding a field of trees in which we deduce that all are mundanely alike, until we closely and carefully examine. Lord, help us to avoid pre-judging persons and thereby missing the God-given unique beauty in another's life. May we be unified, rather than isolated, in our uniqueness. In Christ's name, Amen.

QUESTIONS AND REFLECTIONS

1. Describe what the following phrases/words mean to you:

    a. Agree to disagree agreeably

    b. Uniqueness makes completeness

    c. Oneness, not sameness

    d. Complementarity

2. Respond to the following quote: "No one person/group holds a monopoly on what is truth or what is right." What does this say, for example, about various Christian denominations?

3. Discuss the difference between "negative competition" and "positive complementarity".

4. "…excellence isn't determined by comparing our score to someone else's. Excellence comes from giving your very best, no matter the score." How does this run counter to our Western culture and our human nature?

5. Reflect upon, and respond to, this quotation: "To authentically affirm a differing opinion from our own necessitates an affirmation of our own opinion as well.

16

JUST LET 'EM GO...AND LET 'EM GROW

"Early in the morning, as he was on his way back to the city, he was hungry. Seeing a fig tree by the road, he went up to it but found nothing on it except leaves. Then he said to it, 'May you never bear fruit again!' Immediately the tree withered" (Matthew 21:18,19).

Whenever I converse with a person who doesn't know about growing Christmas trees they are almost always surprised by the amount of work required. One fellow once commented to me, "I always thought when it comes to growing Christmas trees you plant 'em in the ground and just let 'em go and let 'em grow."

To grow a marketable and quality tree it is never that easy. A fraser fir left on its own will not conform to the shape and quality needed for a Christmas tree. The shaping, fertilizing, cultivating, and spraying of the trees must take place consistently and carefully. The key to getting a good final product is getting off to a good start.

Christmas tree farmers cannot expect a good crop of trees if they plant the seedlings in the ground and "let 'em grow" on their own. The young trees require regular and routine maintenance and guidance from the very beginning. A neglected Christmas tree is difficult, if not impossible, especially after several years, to transform and salvage.

So, too, in our lives getting off to a good, solid start physically and spiritually is so important. Spiritually and morally speaking, the values, practices, attitudes and behaviors integrated into our lives during our formative years become the building blocks (whether positive or negative) for the rest of our days.

And, ultimately these building blocks determine how we live and how we die.

A group of tourists were visiting a picturesque village. As they walked through this quaint village they noticed an old man sitting beside a fence. In a rather patronizing way, one tourist asked, "Were any great people born in this village?"

The old man replied, "Nope, only babies."

A patronizing question brought forth a profound answer. There are no instant people or trees. Mature trees and mature people take time to grow. Great persons are not born, they are grown.

♪ Spiritual formation is a process, as well. The Psalmist records: "God blesses those people who refuse evil advice and won't follow sinners or join in sneering at God. Instead, the law of the Lord makes them happy, and they think about it day and night.

They are like trees growing beside a stream, trees that produce fruit in season and out of season and always have leaves. These people succeed in everything they do…" (Psalm 1:1-3, CEV).

One step of faith, grounded and rooted in God, leads to another step of faith…followed by growth. Just as the pine tree grows larger and stronger season by season—nurtured, tended, and shaped by the farmer, so too, as the believer's faith becomes more deeply rooted and firmly grounded, we are enabled to face and withstand the strong storms of life.

As a pastor of many years, I have officiated at hundreds of funerals. Many of the deceased's loved ones were persons of deep resurrection faith—possessing the hope and assurance of eternal life through Jesus Christ. But there were some families, I recall, who did not have this eternal hope. What a contrast!

Those families who were deeply grounded in faith in Jesus Christ—who had assurance that their loved one was in this same care and love of God that they too knew, evidenced a confidence and strength that enabled them to stand strong even in the midst of deep grief and loss!

The strength and resolve that God provides in the midst of our deepest struggle is nothing short of awesome! It is a grace nothing short of amazing! And the outcome of this Christ-based faith is nothing short of blessed assurance!

The beautiful truth of the Christian journey—whether we are experiencing grief or gratitude, agitation or celebration, adversity or prosperity—is that we are never alone. We have the power of God's Holy Spirit within us and the presence of God's people beside us! As a part of the church—the Body of Christ—we have access to, and may tap into, the greatest power in the universe.

Just as the tree planted beside the stream receives all the nourishment it needs to grow strong, so the Christian connected to the church—that community of faith, fellowship, and service in Jesus name—will bring forth fruit for the kingdom of God. Sometimes, surprisingly, amazing "fruit" results, as the community of faith stays rooted and grounded in God's word and will.

David Huxley owns a world record in an unusual category: he pulls jetliners.

On October 15, 1997, for example, he broke his own record at Mascot Airport in Sydney, Australia. He strapped around his upper torso a harness that was attached to a steel cable some fifteen yards long. The other end of the steel cable was attached to the front-wheel strut of a 747 jetliner that weighed 187 tons. With his tennis shoes firmly planted on the runway, Huxley leaned forward, pulled with all his might, and remarkably was able to get the jetliner rolling down the runway. In fact, he pulled the 747 one hundred yards in one minute and twenty seconds. A superhuman feat indeed.

The church resembles that 747 jetliner. The strength of a few extraordinary humans can pull the institution of the church for very short distances. Or we can pray until God starts up powerful engines that enable his church to fly thousands of miles on the wings of the Holy Spirit.

The "fruit", the growth, and the progress occurs in our life because a gracious and patient God sees potential in us and so continues to work on us, in us, and through us. God keeps working to smooth out our rough edges and sand away those sharp corners until we begin to look more and more like our Creator.

Created in the image of God, our sinful, self-centered ways have marred that once-perfect reflection. Yet, God through Christ, offers us a reconciled relationship, a restored image.

As the Christmas tree farmer shears away anything on the tree that doesn't conform to a Christmas tree, so, too, our Master Creator carves away anything that does not conform to the God-image.

As Christians our lives ought to reflect Christ. As disciples of Jesus we should attempt to live like Jesus. And as followers of Christ we are to be transformed by Christ. This transformation process—a continual conversion—can happen only by the initiation and direction of God through His Holy Spirit.

Yet, God in his gracious consideration of humankind's free choice will not force His divine will upon us. So the spiritual growth, or sanctification, process is a divine-human team venture.

We (humanity) cannot redeem our lives nor re-direct ourselves in the way we should go. God (sovereignty) will not work this redemption and redirection process without our cooperation—cooperation with God and cooperation with God's people.

There is no such thing as a "self—made Christian". That term is by definition an oxymoron. Christians, like Christmas trees, when left to grow on their own become unruly, unreliable, and unsuitable for their design and calling.

PRAYER: Master Creator, we praise you for not allowing us to go and grow on our own! Instead, loving God that you are, you have come to us and made a way for us so that there is purpose and direction to our days.

Lord, you know we require so much tending and nurturing and shaping, but you continue to patiently and mercifully offer us your very best care. Forgive us for going our own way. Help us to grow to be more and more like you, finding our God-image restored through Your Son Jesus Christ, in whom we pray, Amen.

QUESTIONS AND REFLECTIONS

1. What would you deem to be the foundational spiritual building blocks in your life?

2. Discuss: "Great persons are not born, they are grown."

3. Read and meditate upon Psalm 1:1-3. What does this passage say about growing spiritually?

4. "The fruit, the growth, and the progress occurs in our lives because a gracious and patient God sees potential in us and so continues to work on us, in us, and through us." Where have you known this to be true?

5. Would you agree that "self-made Christian" is an oxymoron? Why?

17

ROOT ROT

"…If the root is holy, so are the branches" (Romans 11:16b).

An old 4-H motto states: "If you're green you're growing. If you're ripe you're rotting."

One of the reasons you'll likely see faser fir trees growing on the side of a hill or on a slight incline is because they are susceptible to root rot, especially in low-lying, poorly drained areas. They grow, and thrive, much better with proper drainage. A fraser fir with root rot will turn a pale green, or yellow, and probably eventually die a premature death.

Because of what is happening unseen, underground there are adverse effects visible above ground. Due to stagnation and rotting below, the life and vitality of the tree is robbed.

Sometimes our spirits and souls are stymied and stifled, empty and eroded, because we have become stagnant in our spiritual journey.

It is easy for we humans to coast along in life—one day runs into another and we become status quo, never leaving our comfort zone; Never coloring outside the lines. Instead of green and growing we become ripe and rotting. Our God-given dreams die and our goals disappear.

When this "rotting" of our spirits occurs life can seem like a mundane existence rather than a marvelous experience. Life and relationships are taken for granted.

At times, if our spiritual eyes and spirits are open, "wake-up calls" arrive in our lives! Wake-up calls prevent our souls from stagnating and rotting. They are experiences and/or relationships that keep us humble, grateful, and expectant.

At the church where I am presently pastoring we as a congregation had a wake-up call recently. A haggardly homeless man arrived in our city and at our church door. He visited with us one Sunday morning. Took us right out of our comfort zone. We had just recently had a Sunday morning service centering upon Christian hospitality to all people. And then, just a few Sundays later—in walks George!

Our congregation adopted George. Members of our church gave him employment. We made sure he had meals and a secure place to sleep at the local night shelter. One man in our church took George for a haircut and found some clothing for him. Another couple helped George obtain his social security card and other documents.

In talking with George, we found he was from Michigan and had not seen his family in over thirty years, and had not spoken to them in ten years! Some of our members got on-line and were able to locate and communicate with some of George's family during the Fall of the year.

Our church decided to enable George to go home to live with his sisters who were anxiously awaiting his return to reunite with them. We collected the money to pay for his airfare to return home. His sisters would meet him at the airport in their home area.

The Sunday before he flew home, George stood up in front of our congregation and with tears of joy in his eyes, thanked our church family for this gift. The next day George was on a plane and he was home with his family in time for Christmas!

No matter what has happened in our lives. No matter how many knockdowns and failures...with the grace of God and the forgiveness of Christ, there is always opportunity for new beginnings...hope for the future. Every new day, every new moment is a hope-filled opportunity.

A university professor tells of being invited to speak at a military base one December and there meeting an unforgettable soldier named Ralph. Ralph had been sent to meet him at the airport. After they had introduced themselves, they headed toward the baggage claim.

As they walked down the concourse, Ralph kept disappearing. Once to help an older woman whose suitcase had fallen open. Once to lift two toddlers up to where they could see Santa Claus, again to give directions to someone who was lost. Each time he came back with a smile on his face.

"Where did you learn that?" the professor asked.

"What?" Ralph said.

"Where did you learn to give like that?"

"Oh," Ralph said, "during the war, I guess." He then told the professor about his tour of duty in Vietnam, how it was his job to clear mine fields, how he watched his friends blow up before his eyes, one after another.

"I learned to live between steps," he said. "I never knew whether the next one would be my last, so I learned to get everything I could out of the moment between when I picked up my foot and when I put it down again. Every step I took was a whole new world, and I guess I've been that way ever since."

The abundance of our lives is not determined by how long we live, but by how well we live. Keep stepping...keep on keeping on. St. Paul affirms: "I keep on striving, running the race..." Avoid at all costs the stagnant, rotting existence. Of course, there are disappointments. Yes, there will be fumbles and stumbles.

Yet, the powerful promise from Providence is that His almighty hand will keep you from falling. Though we may get knocked down by life's hard knocks, by faith we shall not stay down. Rather, we shall get up and strive and "run and not be weary."

During a Monday night football game between the Chicago Bears and the New York Giants, one of the announcers observed that Walter Payton, the Bears' running back, had accumulated over nine miles in career rushing yardage. The other announcer remarked, "Yeah, and that's with someone knocking him down every 4.6 yards!"

Walter Payton, arguably one of the most successful running backs ever, knew that everyone—even the best—gets knocked down. The key to success, and faithfulness, is to get up and run again just as hard.

Getting up and going forward, one step at a time. Even baby steps are to be celebrated!

With proper planting and adequate drainage faser firs can avoid the life-robbing root rot plague. And, with a proper grounding and a living faith in Christ, human beings can avoid the crippling and crushing effects of a "rotting", dying spirit.

It was a fog-shrouded morning, July 4th, 1952, when a young woman named Florence Chadwick waded into the water off Catalina Island. She intended to swim the channel from the island to the California coast. Long-distance swimming was not new to her; she had been the first woman to swim the English Channel in both directions.

The water was numbing cold that day. The fog was so thick she could hardly see the boats in her party. Several times sharks had to be driven away with rifle fire. She swam more than fifteen hours before she asked to be taken out of the water. Her trainer tried to encourage her to swim on since they were so close to land, but when Florence looked, all she saw was fog. So she quit...only one-half mile from her goal.

Later she said, "I'm not excusing myself, but if I could have seen the land, I might have made it." It wasn't the cold or fear or exhaustion that caused Florence Chadwick to fail. It was the fog.

Many times we too fail, not because we're afraid or because of the peer pressure or because of anything other than the fact that we lose sight of the goal. Maybe that's why Paul said, "I press toward the mark for the prize of the high calling of God in Christ Jesus" (Philippians 3:14).

Two months after her failure, Florence Chadwick walked off the same beach into the same channel and swam the distance, setting a new speed record, because she could see the land.

PRAYER: O Lord, our Lord, you have placed Divinely-directed dreams and God-given goals deep within each of our hearts. Help us to never quit seeking and following your dreams for our lives. Encourage us to not give up on the good goals you have for your kingdom on earth as it is in heaven—goals of righteousness, justice, and peace.

When our days get long and the road gets difficult, Lord, may we not get bogged down in the mire of meaningless mundaneness that only leads to stagnant, rotting results.

Instead, may we soar in the awareness and assurance that we belong to you and you will indeed make a way when there seems to be no way. Enable us, Heavenly Parent, to realize that problems and difficulties that enter our life can be stepping stones instead of roadblocks. We ask this in Christ's name. Amen.

QUESTIONS AND REFLECTIONS

1. What can we do to prevent spiritual stagnation?

2. What "wake-up call" experiences have you encountered?

3. "No matter what has happened in our lives. No matter how many knock-downs and failures...with the grace of God and the forgiveness of Christ there is always opportunity for new beginnings and hope for the future." How do you respond to this statement?

4. Read and discuss Philippians 3:13,14

18

APHID ATTACK

"...I will bring locusts into your country tomorrow...they will devour...including every tree that is growing in your fields" (Exodus 10:4,5).

It is one of the most dreaded statements for a Christmas tree grower to receive: "You have aphids in your trees." Tiny, microscopic-like parasites called aphids have the capability of destroying an entire field(s) of trees if there is no intervention.

The grower must be vigilant in looking for the destructive aphids. And the grower must be diligent in eradicating these pests whenever and wherever they are found. Just because the trees are green and growing does not necessarily mean that aphids are absent.

The beautiful, vibrant green tree may be a deception if these pesky little insects are working havoc on the inside of the tree. If the infested trees are not treated and sprayed with the appropriate pesticide, brown and dead will likely replace green and living.

The presence of aphids in Christmas trees reminds me of at least a couple of principles in life. Number one: How easily and quickly people forget. It seems as if we homo sapiens are slow learners. Whether world history, national history, or our own individual history...we must continue learning the same lessons over and over. We frequently repeat the same, or similar, mistakes. Our memories are short, therefore our time in God's "classroom"—seeking, assimilating and applying divine wisdom—ought to be often and at length.

Scores of people lost their lives. The world's mightiest army was forced to abandon a strategic base. Property damage approached a billion dollars. All because the sleeping giant, Mount Pinatube in the Philippines, roared back to life after six hundred years of quiet slumber.

When asked to account for the incredible destruction caused by this volcano, a research scientist from the Philippines Department of Volcanology observed, "When a volcano is silent for many years, our people forget that it's a volcano and begin to treat it like a mountain."

Like Mount Pinatube, our sinful nature always has the potential to erupt, bringing great harm both to ourselves and to others. The biggest mistake we can make is to ignore the volcano, forgetting what it's potential power can do, and move back onto what seems like a dormant "mountain."

How quickly we forget and often reject God's wise and helpful guidance. We develop spiritual amnesia and selective hearing. This refusal to listen and learn begins in small, seemingly insignificant ways, not unlike the tiny aphid. And, like the aphids destruction of trees…the failure to hear and heed divinity has destructive and catastrophic consequences for our lives.

Which describes principle number two: Small, everyday steps and decisions lead to large, life-changing consequences. These consequences can be, of course, negative or positive, depending upon our choices.

Paul Harvey, radio commentator, relates the story of how Eskimo hunters catch and kill the wild wolf. The hunter places a knife in the ice—blade up. He then coats the knife blade with animal's blood. The hungry wolf finds the knife and begins licking the blood off the blade. As it laps more and more feverishly it doesn't realize it soon is losing it's own blood as the wolf's tongue continues to strike the sharp knife.

What began as a very pleasurable experience for the wolf, with an expected pleasant consequence and outcome, turned out with the wolf lying dead in the snow.

If we build our life upon "shaky ground" and "sinking sand" the consequences are detrimental and even sometimes deadly. But, if we build upon the true and right and solid, we will discover positive outcomes.

A TV news camera crew was on assignment in southern Florida filming the widespread destruction of Hurricane Andrew.

In one scene, amid the devastation and debris stood one house on its foundation. The owner was cleaning up the yard when a reporter approached him.

"Sir, why is your house the only one still standing?" asked the reporter. "How did you manage to escape the severe damage of the hurricane?"

"I built this house myself," the man replied. "I also built it according to the Florida state building code. When the code called for 2 X 6 roof trusses, I used 2 X 6 roof trusses. I was told that a house built according to code could withstand a hurricane. I did, and it did. I suppose no one else around here followed the code."

When the sun is shining and the skies are blue, building our lives on something other than the guidelines in God's Word can be tempting. But there's only one way to be ready for a storm.

Even as the Christmas tees appear healthy, the wise grower must remain on guard, for the annoying microscopic aphids may be already doing devastating damage. Yet, when monitored the aphids may not only be eradicated, but can serve as a motivation for the grower to watch the trees more closely so that the result is a healthier, lovelier product than even before!

This pro-active approach by the farmer can re-frame the annoying, attacking aphid into an opportunity to be more vigilant and careful while growing the trees, so that the end result is a more quality Christmas tree.

Farmers in southern Alabama were accustomed to planting one crop every year—cotton. They would plow as much ground as they could and plant their crop. Year after year they lived by cotton.

Then one year the dreaded boll weevil devastated the whole area. So the next year the farmers mortgaged their homes and planted cotton again, hoping for a good harvest. But as the cotton began to grow, the insect came back and destroyed the crop, wiping out most of the farms.

The few who survived those two years of the boll weevil decided to experiment the third year, so they planted something they'd never planted before—peanuts. And peanuts proved so hardy and the market proved so ravenous for that product that the farmers who survived the first two years reaped profits that third year that enabled them to pay off all their debts. They planted peanuts from then on and prospered greatly.

Then you know what those farmers did? They spent some of their new wealth to erect in the town square a monument—to the boll weevil. If it hadn't been for the boll weevil, they never would have discovered peanuts. They learned t hat even out of disaster positives can result, if the attitudes and the actions are right.

PRAYER: Very often, Lord, it's not the so-called big, obvious temptations and sins that entrap us. No, it's the small, unassuming, deceptive stuff that gets us! Like tiny microscopic aphids attacking a pine tree, so the small everyday choices and decisions that we make regularly have the potential to do catastrophic damage—eventually!

But, these same small decisions can also be wise ones…good choices…that build the character of Christ into our lives. Help us, Lord, to have long spiritual memories, thereby remembering who we are and Whose we are.

Forgive us our selfish, sinful choices, and help us be vigilant and diligent in our service to God and our neighbors. Through Christ we pray, Amen.

QUESTIONS AND REFLECTIONS

1. "The grower (of Christmas trees) must be vigilant in looking for the destructive aphids. And, the grower must be diligent in eradicating these pests whenever and wherever they are found." As for the Christmas tree farmer, why are being vigilant and diligent essential elements of the Christian faith?

2. In what ways have you participated in "spiritual amnesia" and "selective hearing" with God?

3. Where have you observed examples of small, everyday decisions leading to large, life-changing decisions?

19

ʹEVERGREENS

"…I am like a green pine tree; your fruitfulness comes from me" (Hosea 14:8b).

"For the wages of sin is death, but the gift of God is eternal life in Christ Jesus our Lord" (Romans 6:23). "Instead of the thornbush will grow the pine tree, and instead of briers the myrtle will grow. This will be for the Lord's renown, for an everlasting sign, which will not be destroyed."(Isaiah 55:13).

One of the beautiful and unique characteristics of pine trees is their year-round constant green color. Thus, the name evergreen. While all the other trees are changing their colors and even losing their leaves, the pine tree maintains its color throughout the entire year—through all the seasons.

* The pine tree presents a picture of permanence. The evergreen can remind us of that which is eternal.

In a world filled with the temporal, it is wonderful to know a permanence lies ahead. In a world of brokenness and chaos, it is comforting to know a world of perfection and peace is in our future. In a world of weariness and woe, it is re-assuring to realize a perfect rest awaits those who place their trust in the Lord!

On the final page of the final book of The Chronicles of Narnia, some of the children who have been to Narnia lament that they once again must return to their homeland—the Shadow-Lands. But Aslan (the lion who represents Jesus) has the best news of all for them:

"{Aslan spoke to the children,} 'You do not yet look so happy as I mean you to be."

Lucy said, 'We're so afraid of being sent away, Aslan. And you have sent us back into our own world so often.'

'No fear of that,' said Aslan. 'Have you not guessed?'

Their hearts leaped and a wild hope rose within them.

'There was a real railway accident,' said Aslan softly. 'Your father and mother and all of you are—as you used to call it in the Shadow-lands—dead. The term is over: the holidays have begun. The dream has ended; this is morning.'

And as he spoke he no longer looked to them like a lion; but the things that began to happen after that were so great and beautiful that I cannot write them. And for us this is the end of all the stories, and we can most truly say that they all lived happily ever after. But for them it was only the beginning of the real story. All their life in this world and all their adventures in Narnia had only been the cover and the title page: now at last they were beginning Chapter One of the Great Story, which on one on earth has read: which goes on forever: in which every chapter is better than the one before." (C.S. Lewis, The Last Battle).

The tremendous truth is that for the follower of Christ eternal life begins here and now, and never ends! As Aslan's words remind us: "[This eternal life] goes on tomorrow: in which every chapter is better than the one before." Believers, therefore, face an endless hope instead of a hopeless end.

As Christians, not only do we possess the hope of a glorious heavenly future, but the hope of seeing and participating in God's justice and mercy carried out "here and now"—as we have been taught to pray—"Thy will be done on earth as it is in heaven."

The hopeful vision of the future and the "here and now" action are permanently wed for the follower of Christ.

"The hope of a glorious, ideal future is neither a 'crutch' on which we lean until we experience the glory of God nor a 'carrot' that we futilely strive after while wearing blinders so that we avoid seeing the needs of those around us. Instead, the kingdom of God, and the glory of God, is to be experienced and promoted 'on earth as it is in heaven' (Matthew 6:10). While we anticipate a complete revelation of God's glory, we also participate in the glimpses of God's glory that we are afforded." (p. 74, Michael D. Kurtz, Approaching the New Millennium)

Authentic Christianity breeds ethical and social transformation. The promise of a perfect future offers us "anticipatory hope," but glimpses of God's kingdom on earth motivate us to "participatory hope."

During his presidential election campaign, John F. Kennedy frequently closed his speeches with a story about Colonel Davenport, the Speaker of the Connecticut House of Representatives. On an ominously dark day in Hartford, some of the legislators looked out the windows and feared the end was at hand. As they began demanding immediate adjournment, Davenport stood and stated, "The Day of Judgment is either approaching or it is not. If it is not, there is no cause for adjournment. If it is, I choose to be found doing my duty. Therefore, I wish that candles be brought."

Like Colonel Davenport we must call for candles and let our lights shine. Rather than fearing the darkness, we are to be faithful until Christ ushers in his final kingdom. Instead of being paranoid about the future, we are to let our lights shine as we watch and wait. It is comforting to note that the light shines brightest in the darkest environment.

We are instructed through the Great Commission, "Go therefore and make disciples of al nations, baptizing them in the name of the Father and of the Son and of the Holy Spirit, and teaching them to obey everything that I have commanded you. And remember, I am with you always to the end of the age" (Matthew 28:19-20). Notice the action words (verbs) Jesus intentionally employs—"go," "baptizing," "teaching," "remember."

As Christians, we are to study, to analyze, and to take inventory of the needs in our world. It is crucial that we do our homework. However, there comes a time when we must step out with an active faith that remembers Christ will be with us "to the end of the age." Otherwise, we run the danger of the "paralysis of analysis" syndrome. Our Christian faith affirms that those who are most hopeful over the next world are the most involved in this world.

As we behold the evergreen trees may we be reminded and reassured that God's gift of eternal life is within us and while the fullness of eternal life is not totally realized, one day it will be realized and received beyond our wildest imagination…"Every chapter better than the one before!"

PRAYER: Eternal God, you are the Source of all life—physical and spiritual. In you we move and have our being. Thank you for the glimpses of eternal, resurrection life we see and experience in this world. These glimpses, O God, are only a foretaste of the glorious forever when there will be no more injustice, no more suffering, and no more dying. In the name of our Savior and Lord we are promised an endless hope. Amen.

QUESTIONS AND REFLECTIONS

1. "The tremendous truth is that for the follower of Christ eternal life begins here and now and never ends!" Some theologies and denominations focus almost exclusively on heaven by and by; others dwell almost constantly on social justice here and now. We should not fall prey to the tyranny of the "either—or". Rather, it is a both—and. What is your response to this "tremendous truth"?

2. In what ways does the prayer Jesus taught us to pray (The Lord's Prayer) incorporate "here and now" and "then and there" faith? For example, "Thy kingdom come, Thy will be done on earth as it is in heaven."

3. Discuss the following quotation: "Authentic Christianity breeds ethical and social transformation."

20

FRASER FIRS GROW BEST IN THE HIGH COUNTRY

"You will go out in joy and be led forth in peace; the mountains and hills will burst into song before you, and all the trees of the field will clap their hands" (Isaiah 55:12).

"You can take the boy out of the mountains but you can't take the mountains out of the boy." So goes an old quote.

As a mountain boy—reared in the northwest mountains of North Carolina—I find this to be true. No matter how far away I go, or how long I stay, the call of my mountain home keeps calling and bringing me back. Mountains represent, for me strength, security, a slower pace of life, and a natural serenity.

My wife's late granddad—a wise and gentle mountain man, would sometimes visit and stay a night or two in "the flatlands" with his relatives. But two nights was the limit because in his own words, "I've gotta get back to the mountains so I can have something to rest my eyes against."

The mountains were good for Granddad's health. He just was at home and did better in the high country.

So do fraser firs. In fact, the fraser fir grows naturally only in the southern Appalachians, above 3000 feet. The cool temperatures and plentiful rainfall of the North Carolina high country are what causes the faser fir to retain its needles throughout the Christmas Season.

As my pen finds this page on a hot, humid day in an urban area of the North Carolina Piedmont, my heart pines for the cooler, cleaner air of the North Carolina hills—a place where there is room to breathe and stretch and grow and go higher.

In our spiritual walk we need to go higher…deeper…in the faith.

Notice the words to an old hymn of the Christian faith by Johnson Oatman, Jr. entitled "Higher Ground":

I'm pressing on the upward way, new heights I'm gaining every day; Still praying as I onward bound, 'Lord plant my feet on higher ground.

My heart has no desire to stay Where doubts arise and fears dismay; Though some may dwell where these abound, My prayer, my aim is higher ground.

I want to live above the world, Though Satan's darts at me are hurled; For faith has caught the joyful sound, The song of saints on higher ground.

I want to scale the utmost height And catch a gleam of glory bright; But still I'll pray till heav'n I've found, 'Lord lead me on to higher ground.'

Chorus: Lord, lift me up and let me stand, By faith, on heaven's tableland, a higher plane than I have found; Lord, plant my feet on higher ground.

We need the nourishment of the high country in our spiritual walk. We require the decisions of the "high road" in our choices. Do you know why the notorious bears of Yellowstone National Park aren't as visible as they used to be? Well, it seems that over the years these furry creatures were not only being photographed by wide-eyed tourists, they were also being fed. And the food offered the bears was quite different from their natural diets of nuts, berries, fish, and small animals. The resulting consequences were tragic.

During hibernation the fat buildup from "people food" burned off much more rapidly than the normal animal fat created by a bear's natural diet. Throughout the winter months, scores of bruins froze to death. So the remaining bears were relocated by trucks to the high country, away from the trail of tourists.

I wonder how many of us need to be relocated to the high country where our daily diet of discipleship can be assured. In the same way that the bears must be guarded against the wrong kind of food, so we must guard against the wrong kind of spiritual diet.

Like the Yellowstone bears freezing to death in their winter sleep, Christians who have eaten the wrong kind of food have little inner resources on which to rely when faced with personal storms.

Nothing can take the place of firsthand study of the Bible and personal communication with God in prayer and meditation. No one can live our faith for us. Christianity cannot be lived vicariously through a pastor, a best friend, or anyone else.

God created us to be nourished personally and corporately through his Word, just as he intended the bears in Yellowstone National Park to eat from his creation. As the bear which is properly nourished survives the winter, the Christian who is nourished by God's words withstands the winters of life.

In our spiritual journey, God calls us to go higher and grow deeper in the faith…to move from the milk of the baby to the meat of the mature. To the spiritually immature Christians at Corinth, Paul writes: "…I could not address you as spiritual but as worldly—mere infants in Christ. I gave you milk, not solid food, for you were not yet ready for it. Indeed, you are still not ready" (I Corinthians 3:1,2).

As disciples of Jesus Christ we are to be weaned from the bottle and move on to bigger and better things—growing more and more mature in the faith. We are to "rise above" (take higher ground) the pettiness and mediocrity of others. After all, we are representing Christ to others. We must be distinct or we will become extinct.

Discipleship is about a higher calling. This is not the route of least resistance, rather it is the way of faith and persistence. As our "faith roots" go deeper we will grow stronger and reach higher and further.

In the words of Douglas Wood:

"I've always been in love with pines. The massive, reaching limbs, the silhouettes, the way they cradle the stars at night. The smell of fallen needles carpeting the earth. When I was very young, the big pines looked to me as if they grew by simply grabbing a hold of the sky and hauling themselves up out of the earth.

Later I learned some simple things about life. I am still learning them. That pines…and dandelions and people…grow from where they are rooted. From the bottom up. From the inside out. That growth is slow. That grasping the air just means being toppled by the wind."

Growing from where we are rooted…blooming from where we are planted…may we as God's people go deeper into the Word so that we may go further into the world—going higher and reaching wider.

Sometimes our vision gets so near-sighted. There is so much God has in store for us, yet our "reductionistic faith" places limits and blinders on our God-given potential! If only we could see through God's eyes! A divine-perspective is required…a "higher plane" is necessary. Our human perspective is finite and limited. But God sees it all. And, God's ways are not our ways.

The Apostle Paul writes: "But do not ignore this one fact, beloved, that with the Lord one day is like a thousand years, and a thousand years are like one day" (2 Peter 3:8 NRSV).

An economist who read this passage was quite amazed and talked to God about it. "Lord, is it true that a thousand years for us is like one minute to you?"

The Lord said yes.

The economist said, "Then a million dollars to us must be like one penny to you."

The Lord said, "Well, yes."

The economist said, "Will you give me one of those pennies?"

The Lord said, "All right, I will. Wait here a minute."

How grateful we should be for receiving even glimpses of God's vision for our lives! For as we see more and more through the eyes of faith, seeking higher ground, we become more and more blessed so that we may be a blessing to others.

As I walk through this high country field of faser firs, I thank God for mountain top experiences—literally, but much more so for spiritual ones.

Thank God for those mountain top experiences! I have found they do not come that often and they don't come easily; they don't arrive without persistent climbing and expending effort. But they always provide us perspective and inspiration for living.

Faser fir trees grow best in the high country. God's children grow strongest by following closely the high call of God in Christ Jesus.

PRAYER: Righteous and Holy God, we settle for less than best. We are content to rest in the flat land, when you are calling us to climb to higher ground. On the higher ground we gain perspective for our days. Help us, O Lord, to go higher in our spiritual journey. Let us not be satisfied with status quo. Rather, inspire us to go deeper in the faith than we ever have before. Lead us to eat fully at your table and to drink deeply of your cup...so that it runs over and spills out into the lives of others. So that they will experience and know your goodness and mercy and love. In the Name above all names, we pray, Amen.

QUESTIONS AND REFLECTIONS

1. Read out loud and talk about the words to the hymn "Higher Ground".

2. Discuss I Corinthians 3:1,2.

3. "As disciples of Jesus Christ we are to 'rise above' the pettiness and mediocrity of others." How does this philosophy relate to our daily living?

4. Respond to the following quotation: "We must be distinct or we will become extinct."

5. What are some ways you have discovered that better enable you to "see through the eyes of faith"?

6. Recall, and give God thanks for, some mountain top experiences in your life journey.

21

' *TOO MUCH SHADE*

"The people walking in darkness have seen a great light; on those living in the land of the shadow of death a light has dawned" (Isaiah 9:2).

"For you were once darkness, but now you are light in the Lord. Live as children of light (for the fruit of the light consists in all goodness, righteousness and truth)" (Ephesians 5:8).

The first crop of Christmas trees planted was a learning experience. A trial-and-error motif. For instance, several trees were planted in shady areas—in the shadows of a nearby forest. The result? Several trees that were dwarfed in size and dull in color.

Because of our poor location selection the process of plant photosynthesis was severely handicapped for these shaded pines. Christmas trees need ample amounts of sunshine in order to grow strong and healthy.

We, likewise, require God's light shining in our souls and through our spirits in order to grow spiritually strong and healthy. The prophet Isaiah writes: "Come…let us walk in the light of the Lord" (Isaiah 2:5).

John, in his Epistle, affirms: "This is the message we have heard from him and declare to you: God is light; in him there is no darkness at all. If we claim to have fellowship with him yet walk in the darkness, we lie and do not live by the truth. But if we walk in the light as he is in the light, we have fellowship with one another, and the blood of Jesus, his Son, purifies us from all sin" (I John 1:5-7).

Living in the darkness delivers deadly consequences. Life in darkness leads to "dark deeds", cover-ups, damaging secrets and unhealthy denials.

O February 9, 1996, a railroad train running from Waldwick, New Jersey, to Hoboken ran through a red signal and smashed into the side of another train at a crossing. The crash killed the engineers of both trains and one passenger, and injured 158 other passengers.

One year later the National Transportation Safety Board announced the results of its investigation into the cause of the accident. The engineer of the train that ran the red signal was going blind. According to Matthew Wald in the "New York Times", for nine years the engineer had progressively been going blind because of diabetes. He and his doctor both knew it. But he had kept his medical condition a secret, no doubt for fear of losing his work, and the doctor, who reportedly knew that his patient was a railroad engineer, had not reported the man's condition to the railroad.

New Jersey requires that its engineers have a physical exam each year by the company's own occupational medicine specialist, but each year the engineer had "always answered no to the annual questions about whether he had diabetes, was taking any prescription medication or was under another doctor's care. He had had eye surgery twice, but apparently paid for it out of pocket rather than filing insurance claims," says Wald. Unfortunately, the truth came out in a deadly way. Some things we must not keep secret.

Living in God's light leads to a life of liberation and love. The light exposes, sometimes painfully, our shadow side. Yet, it is this painful exposure that can lead us to confession and reformation, essential steps in the process of healing and wholeness.

On a warm, summer night a husband and wife were traveling in their car with their three-year-old son Micah in the back seat. After many miles of driving in the darkness, they came to a stop in a remote area. The brightness of the traffic light revealed all of the dirt, dead bugs, and insects on the car windshield. Micah said, "Look, how dirty!"

Micah's parents didn't think much of their son's comment until a moment later as they drove on…away from the light and back into the darkness. Upon reentering the darkness, they could no longer see the mess on their windshield, and Micah quickly piped up and said, "Now the glass is clean!"

Before the law came, the dirt within us hid under the darkness. But when God gave the law, its light shined on the windshield of our hearts and revealed the filth of sin we'd collected on our journey. The law, then, is a light that shows us how sinful we really are. It cannot cleanse us or make us whole. But it does starkly highlight the true situation of our souls—and can therefore lead us to Christ.

The darkness of Satan saturates our sphere. But, Jesus Christ, the Light of the world, has overcome—overcome the darkness of hatred with the light of love; the darkness of evil with the light of goodness.

We have a choice. We may choose darkness, or we may choose light. Because we are created in the image of God—imago Deo—we have a "light" side in our souls. We are drawn toward the true light of the world. Yet, because of our fallen human nature, original sin and personal sin, we also possess a "shadow" side. The "light" and the "shadow" sides are at war. A conflict rages in our soul! Who will deliver us from this critical conflict?

Thanks be to God…who through Christ Jesus has overcome evil with good and overcome darkness with his great light! Let us choose the way of Light and leave the ways of darkness.

Back when electricity was first being introduced to a little Scottish village, almost everybody in a particular church switched from the propane lanterns to electricity just as soon as it could be hooked up. However, the oldest couple in the congregation couldn't get their electricity because they were waiting for the poles to go up and the wire to be strung. So they continued to use their propane lanterns.

The day finally came when the electricity was brought into their home. Everyone came for the festive event. The old man waited for it to get extra dark; then he told his wife to go turn on the switch. When she did, the light filled the room, and everyone rejoiced. The old man grinned from ear to ear, picked up a propane lamp and said, "It sure makes lighting my lamp easier." And with that he lit a lamp, and his wife turned off the electricity.

Sometimes we're just like that. We can't see the light for need to hang on to the darkness in our life. As one person put it, we have "eyes that grope in a fog that never lifted."

Through God's enlightening grace we no longer must live in the dark! The fog is lifted as we know the true Source of light. God will illumine the way for us through the darkness.

A father and mother took their eleven-year-old son and seven-year-old daughter to Carlsbad Caverns. As always, when the tour reached the deepest point in the cavern, the guide turned off all the lights to dramatize how completely dark and silent it is below the earth's surface.

The little girl, suddenly enveloped in utter darkness, was frightened and began to cry.

Immediately was heard the voice of her brother, "Don't cry. Somebody here knows how to turn on the lights."

In a real sense, that is the message of the gospel: light is available, even when darkness seems overwhelming.

The next time we planted a new crop of Christmas trees, our planting error taught us a valuable lesson. This time we made sure that no trees were planted in the shade so that they would receive the light that leads to life and health.

PRAYER: Light of the world, shine in us and shine through us. Remove the "shadow" side of our selves so that we become authentic and whole. Sometimes our waywardness gets us into dark cavernous places. Forgive us! And as we seek the light of your face, Lord, thank you that your light shines forth in the darkness and you rescue us! We pray as your confident children, for the Light has come into the world and the darkness will never put out the Light! In Jesus name we pray, Amen.

QUESTIONS AND REFLECTIONS

1. Sometimes our poor location decisions lead to "shady" choices. Explain.

2. Read and reflect upon I John 1:5-7.

3. Respond to the following quotation: "Living in God's light leads to a life of liberation and love. The light exposes, sometimes painfully, our shadow side. Yet, it is this painful exposure that can lead us to…wholeness."

4. What are some evidences that we humans possess a "light" side. And, what are some signs that we possess a "shadow" side?

5. What is the ultimate solution to the human "tug-of-war" between our "light" side and our "shadow" side?

22

RIDDING OF THE WEEDS

"Cursed is the ground because of you; through painful toil you will eat of it all the days of your life. It will produce thorns and thistles for you, and you will eat the plants of the field" (Genesis 3:17b).

Keeping weeds out of the Christmas tree fields is one of the toughest jobs. Weeds that grow and mature rob seedlings of essential sunlight and nutrients necessary to the trees' healthy development.

Therefore, every spring, summer, and fall season would find us mowing and spraying and cutting weeds out of the fields. To do this correctly the grower has to be vigilant and persistent.

Nagging, life-sapping weeds are an appropriate metaphor for sin—sin that nags at us and saps life from our souls.

The world as God created it was Paradise—the perfect place to be. Humankind was in complete harmony with God, with one another, and with the earth. Harmony existed in the beginning because humanity did not attempt to usurp God's role, to deceive one another, or to exploit the earth.

Humankind's rebellion against God caused the perfect harmony to disintegrate. The garden of Eden, and the world, was no longer a perfect place to call home. Adam and Eve wanted to set their own agendas. Ever since, human beings have striven to place themselves on the throne.

The result of this self-centeredness is reflected in the Greek word "hubris", meaning "shame" or "injury." Because of our attempt to play God, we hurt (injure) God, others, and ourselves; and the consequences of this sin are manifested.

Look at the sobering words Adam hears from God in Genesis 3:17-19:

"To Adam he said, "Because you listened to your wife and ate from the tree about which I commanded you, 'You must not eat of it,' Cursed is the ground because of you; through painful toil you will eat of it all the days of your life. It will produce thorns and thistles for you, and you will eat the plants of the field. By the sweat of your brow you will eat your food until you return to the ground, since from it you were taken; for dust you are and to dust you will return."

"It [the ground] will produce thorns and thistles for you…" Thorns are now a part of the garden. Thistles are upon the landscape. Crabgrass is growing rampant. Weeds are out of control!

If you are a gardener, you can relate to all of this. A few years ago I had a tough battle with crabgrass in my vegetable garden. I think the stuff can take root on concrete in the middle of a desert with zero annual rainfall. I chopped and chopped, trying to keep the greedy grass off my beans. I kept it away only by ripping it out by the roots and discarding it.

I imagine Adam must have deeply regretted eating that forbidden fruit every time he hoed a thistle or destroyed a thorn or battled weeds.

How about you? Are there any "thorns" in your life that need to be removed? We all have those areas that need weeding and cultivating. Because of our first parents (Adam and Eve) and because of our biological parents and because of our own irresponsible choices, sin is a part of our everyday world. To deny this is to deny reality. The "New England Primer" put it well: "In Adam's fall we sinned all." Scripture reminds us of this painful truth: "All have sinned and fall short of the glory of God" (Romans 3:23).

Were it not for the loving mercy of a gracious Gardener, we would be forever doomed to the plague of "thorns." Because of God's miraculous plan of atonement, however, we do not have to grovel under the overbearing weight of our sin. We are offered a way out of our misery…a way out of our messy weeds! And the way is free! Yet the acceptance of this atonement calls for the sacrifice of our entire life. We cannot fully comprehend this way. It does not make sense from the human perspective that the divine benefactor would erase the sin in our life for no other reason than that God loves us unconditionally. Nonetheless, while God's acceptance cannot be fathomed, it can be assimilated and experienced in our life. What an amazing wonder that is! The kind of things we have done to God, to others, even to ourselves—How could we find forgiveness? Is it possible that God loves us? The answer is that it is not only possible, it is definite. God's love goes out to all people everywhere.

The loving Gardener intercedes and intervenes on our behalf. God is full of mercy toward us, and God's love is over-flowing. By God's grace we are rescued from spiritual death and despair. As has been aptly stated, "Grace is getting what we don't deserve. Mercy is not getting what we deserve."

Once again humankind is afforded the opportunity of being in harmony with God. The gracious Gardener who created "in the beginning" the perfect habitat has lovingly intervened to replace our brokenness with wholeness, our estrangement with restoration!

PRAYER: Gracious Gardener, because of our resistance of you we find ourselves in "thorny" predicaments. Because of our rebellion against you we discover we are entangled in sin's web. By the power of your grace and mercy, remove the pesky, painful "thorns" from our life. Through your love and compassion rid us of the weedy webs of life. And, in your Son Jesus Christ make us one with you, O Lord, and one with each other! Amen.

QUESTIONS AND REFLECTIONS

1. "Adam and Eve wanted to set their own agenda. Ever since, human beings have striven to place themselves on the throne." In what ways do you see this condition manifest in our human experience?

2. Compare and contrast "original sin" and "personal sin."

3. What "thorns" and "thistles" do you face?

4. Thankfully, in our weedy, thorny life a loving Gardener intercedes and intervenes on our behalf! Describe this divine intervention.

5. Discuss: "Grace is getting what you don't deserve. Mercy is not getting what we do deserve."

HARVESTING

23

YOU CAN RUN, BUT YOU CANNOT HIDE

"Then the man and his wife heard the sound of the Lord God as he was walking in the garden in the cool of the day, and they hid from the Lord God among the trees of the garden" (Genesis 3:8).

One of our human tendencies is to hide. Our very first parents, as a result of their rebelliousness against God, hid. And we have been hiding ever since.

We run. We hide. We make excuses for our behaviors. We rationalize. We employ all kinds of mental defenses and psychological ploys in an effort to deny and avoid the painful truth that we have sin in our life.

We have even taken "sin" out of our vocabulary and substituted euphemisms such as: "dysfunction" and "mistake." Our verbal confusion and delusion deepens with our increasing practice of "doublespeak." In a book entitled "The New Doublespeak: Why No One Knows What Anyone's Saying Anymore," writer William Lutz shares some of the more creative, and popular terms:

-meaningful downturn in aggregate output (recession)

-after-sales service (kickback)

-resource development park (trash dump)

-temporarily displaced inventory (stolen goods)

-strategic misrepresentation (lie)

-reality augmentation (lie)

-terminological inexactitude (lie)

Our creative juices flow like fountains when facing honest personal inventory and accountability! We expend all kinds of energy and resources attempting to defend ourselves, even, no especially, when we are in the wrong.

It is amazing how we delude ourselves into thinking we can "hide" and even get away with our sinfulness and wrongdoing! Yet, sooner or later it does catch up with us. We will eventually reap what we sow. In the words of an old oil filter advertisement: "You can pay me now or you can pay me later." Our sin does not just go away and dissipate. Hopefully we will come out of our denial, confess our sin before God, and experience the freeing grace of Jesus Christ. Thankfully, we can experience this liberating love of the Lord today.

A friend and fellow tree-grower of mine shared with me an incident that happened to him that illustrates our human tendency to deceive others and excuse ourselves.

Carl told me he was out in his fields doing some rabbit hunting with his shotgun in hand. He was walking quietly through some of his Christmas trees when he noticed, across several rows, a man with an axe cutting one of Carl's beautiful seven-foot fraser firs. The guy didn't have a clue that Carl was around and watchin'. So, he chopped away until the big tree fell.

Carl walked up to this stranger in his field and casually started a conversation. "How you doin?" "Fine. Just gettin' me a Christmas tree. I've been choppin' one down for the past three or four years and the guy don't even seem to miss 'em."

At this point Carl had lost his patience with this thief. So he pointed his shotgun in his face and demanded: "I happen to own these trees and I appreciate you letting me know about the past several years. Now, buddy, how 'bout getting some money out of your wallet and payin' me for this tree plus the three you chopped in previous years!"

Carl said the guy took out his wallet, gave him all the cash he had, turned around and walked out of the field. He has not seen the man since that day.

What a rude awakening! On a cold winter's day, in the middle of a Christmas tree field, a man's thievery was exposed, and a man's rationalizations were rendered null and void. This man was reaping that which he sowed.

We can all be thankful if a "Carl" or a "Carla" helps us come out of our rationalization and denial! God could use that person in your life just as Nathan was used in David's life. The prophet Nathan confronted King David about his adulterous and murderous behavior, and the result was confession and restoration with God!

Let's come clean. Let's be real. Let's cut out the lame excuses. Confess. And find forgiveness and wholeness.

Former great coach of the Miami Dolphins, Don Shula, tells of losing his temper on the sidelines while near an open microphone during a televised game against the Los Angeles Rams. Millions of viewers were shocked by Shula's explicit profanity. Letters began arriving from all over the country, expressing the disappointment of many who had respected the coach for his integrity.

Shula could have given excuses, but he didn't. Everyone who included a return address received a personal apology. He closed each letter by stating: "I value your respect and will do my best to earn it again."

There are two ways to gain respect. One is to act nobly. The other is, when you fail to do so, make no excuses.

A life of integrity is not a life of perfection. Rather, it is a life of authenticity. It is a life that does not engage in pretension. It does not participate in hiding. It is a life that does not run from the truth.

Instead, it is a life that accepts and embraces the grace-gift of God and shares that grace with others. This amazing grace-gift enables and empowers us to not hide from the truth…and not even run from the truth. For the truth will set you free! Living in deceit equals a dead-end.

Coming home from work, a woman stopped at the corner deli to buy a chicken for supper.

The butcher reached into a barrel, grabbed the last chicken he had, flung it on the scales behind the counter, and told the woman its weight.

She thought for a moment. "I really need a bit more chicken than that," she said. Do you have any larger ones?"

Without a word, the butcher put the chicken back into the barrel, groped around as though finding another, pulled the same chicken out, and placed it on the scales. "This chicken weighs one pound more," he announced.

The woman pondered her options and then said, "Okay. I'll take them both."

Deceit is detected sooner or later.

PRAYER: O Holy God, we look at your holiness and we see our sinfulness! And it hurts and embarrasses us. Yet, Lord sometimes because it pains us so much to look at our sin we pretend that it is not there. We deny it. We try to avoid it. We make excuses. But the sin only deepens. The guilt and shame only increase—hopefully, if we have not anesthetized our conscience!

Help us, God, to put aside pretension, help us to root out rationalizing, and help us to eliminate excuses. May we see ourselves as you see us. Bring us to confession that our spirits might be restored and our lives renewed for your kingdom's sake. Amen.

QUESTIONS AND REFLECTIONS

1. Why do we run and hide from the truth?

2. List some of our human defenses that keep us from facing the truth.

3. Do you have a "Nathan" in your life? Are you a "Nathan" to someone else?

4. Define "integrity"

24

THE BAILING BEGINS

"Do not conform any longer to the pattern of this world, but be transformed by the renewing of your mind..." (Romans 12:2a)

It almost seems like there ought to be a religious litany spoken as the motor of the Christmas bailer is cranked and the first cut tree of the Season is placed into its grasp. Somehow this large, sprawling fraser fir is compacted into a size and shape suitable for transporting by automobile to someone's home.

As I watch this transformation process, I am reminded of the scripture which speaks of the "camel going through the eye of a needle."

This bailing procedure is explainable but the outcome is remarkable! Actually...while one worker feeds the tree into the opening mouth of the bailer's cone, another worker attaches a strong cable with claw-like handles to the trunk of the tree, pulling it through the cone. All the while bailer twine is wrapped around the tree until it is conformed in size and shape appropriate for hauling.

The pressure and stress placed upon the tree as it enters the bailer is enormous. Sometimes some of the lower and larger branches are broken because they just will not conform to the bailer's boundaries. And, yet, the limbs that do not comply must be broken off and discarded so that the tree will serve its purpose.

The lesson of the broken tree is applicable to our Christian life. We must be broken before we may be made whole. We must surrender our will to be broken before God. Then it is that we can be shaped more nearly into the image of Christ.

In the words of a hymn: "Have Thine own way, Lord. Have Thine own way. Thou art the Potter, I am the clay. Mold me and make me after Thy will, while I am waiting yielded and still."

God's shaping process is neither quick nor stress free...but it is the way to true peace and joy. As the Christmas tree is shaped and molded by the bailer, so our Christian lives need to be conformed to the yoke of Jesus Christ. Jesus instructs,

"Take my yoke upon you and learn from me, for I am gentle and humble in heart, and you will find rest for your souls" (Matthew 11:29). One version reads, "My yoke is easy..." "Easy" here does not mean without effort. Rather, the term Jesus uses implies that the yoke is easy in the sense that it fits. It is right. It is what we need. It is best for us. Therefore, it fits.

There is a lot of extra and unruly growth that can grow on a Christmas tree to its own detriment...Growth that can make it much more difficult, and sometimes impossible, to adhere to the bailer's specifications and capacities. It is often necessary to get out the axe and shears to remove this "excess baggage" so that the tree will fit in the bailer.

Someone shares that as they walked through a park they passed a massive oak tree. A vine had grown up along its trunk. The vine started small—nothing to bother about. But over the years the vine had gotten taller and taller. By the time this person passed, the entire lower half of the tree was covered by the vine's creepers. The mass of tiny feelers was so thick that the tree looked as though it had innumerable birds' nests in it.

Now the tree was in danger. This huge, solid oak was quite literally being taken over; the life was being squeezed from it.

But the gardeners in that park had seen the danger. They had taken a saw and severed the trunk of the vine—one neat cut across the middle. The tangled mass of the vine's branches still clung to the oak, but the vine was now dead. That would gradually become plain as weeks passed and the creepers began to die and fall away from the tree.

How easy it is for sin, which begins so small and seemingly insignificant, to grow out of control until it has a strangling grip on our lives.

But sin's power is severed by Christ, and gradually, as we yield daily to Christ, and fit into his yoke, sin's grip dries up and falls away...leaving us liberated. The yoke of Christ is easy. It fits!

At harvest time the Christmas tree must submit to the shaping of the bailer. In the Christian walk, the disciple of Christ must yield to the design of the Redeemer.

If we are serious about this Christian-living thing then we must surrender our self-centered wills and egos to the will of God. The Almighty Gardener must provide His nurturing touch and cultivating guidance if our gardens are to survive and thrive.

Someone writes about a business consultant who decided to landscape his grounds. He hired a woman with a doctorate in horticulture who was extremely knowledgeable.

Because the business consultant was very busy and traveled a lot, he kept emphasizing to her the need to create his garden in a way that would require little or no maintenance on his part. He insisted on automatic sprinklers and other labor-saving devices.

Finally she stopped and said, "There's one thing you need to deal with before we go any further. If there's no gardener, there's no garden!"

There are no labor-saving devices for growing a garden of spiritual virtue. Becoming a person of spiritual fruitfulness—shaped more and more into the image of Christ—requires time, attention, care and constant submission into the loving and guiding hands of the Gracious Gardener.

PRAYER: Dear Heavenly Parent, we resist your shaping process. Yet our souls hunger for your guiding design in our lives. Teach us the wisdom of recognizing that your "yoke is easy." And grant us the courage to entrust our lives completely into the Hands that created us and continue to create us each day of our lives. In Christ's name we pray, Amen.

QUESTIONS AND REFLECTIONS

1. Discuss the Christian paradox that you must be broken before you may be made whole.

2. Read and respond to Matthew 11:29.

3. The Christian-shaping process is constant! Give your responses to the following quotation: "If we are serious about this Christian-living thing then we must surrender our self-centered wills and egos to the will of God. The Almighty Gardener must provide His nurturing touch and cultivating guidance if our gardens are to survive and thrive."

25

WHAT'S IN A NAME?

"O Christmas Tree"

(O Tannenbaum)

O Christmas tree, O Christmas tree! Thou tree most fair and lovely!
The sight of thee at Christmastide, Spreads hope and gladness far and wide.
O Christmas tree, O Christmas tree! Thou tree most fair and lovely.

O Christmas tree, O Christmas tree! Thou hast a wondrous message:
Thou dost proclaim the Savior's birth, Good will to men and peace on earth.
O Christmas tree, O Christmas tree! Thou hast a wondrous message.

E. G. Anschuetz   German Folk Song

Whoever first called pine trees "evergreens" summed it up accurately! All year round—every season—these stately trees add green beauty to landscapes. Their name (evergreen) describes correctly their identity—their constantness…their consistency = Ever; and, their color = Green.

Names can tell us a lot. In the ancient Hebrew culture a person's identity was summed up in their name. For example, "Isaac"—whose parents Abraham and Sarah laughed when God promised they would bear a son in their elderly years—means "laughter". Joshua, leader of and warrior for God's people, means "deliverer".

In our contemporary culture expecting parents often spend much time contemplating and selecting names for their unborn children. Karen and I considered carefully before naming our two children.

Our son—Joshua—has many characteristics and qualities of the strong leader Joshua in the biblical Old Testament. Our daughter—Anna—has many characteristics and qualitites of the prayer warrior, Anna, in the New Testament.

Some choose to name their offspring biblical names. Some choose family names. Others choose names that are pleasing to their ears. Whatever the reason(s)…whatever the motive(s)…there is a lot of meaning in a name.

Names and words carry a lot of meaning and a lot of power and influence. Names and words have the ability to create a negative or a positive environment. For example, Alan Loy McGinnis writes ("Bringing out the Best in People" Minneapolis: Augsburger Publishing House, 1985, p. 35):

"People need an atmosphere in which they can specialize, hone their skills, and discover their distinctiveness. The biographies of the great are sprinkled with accounts of how some teacher of some kindly employer looked closely enough to see a spark no one else saw and for periods, at least, believed in their ability to perfect that gift when no one else did. The Taft family, for instance, was good at pushing their children to cut their own swath and to find a speciality of which to be proud. When Martha Taft was in elementary school in Cincinnati she was asked to introduce herself. She said, 'My name is Martha Bowers Taft. My great grandfather was President of the United States. My grandfather was United States senator. My daddy is ambassador to Ireland. And I am a Brownie.'"

Little Martha Taft was proud of her name—no doubt because she had a family that encouraged and enabled her positive self esteem through assertive actions and affirming words.

In scripture father Isaac speaks words of blessing to his son: "Son, come here and let me bless you." That's a powerful verbal affirmation for the son to hear!

Words are powerful, especially words from someone we really value and respect. Words have the potential of tearing us down or building us up.

Yet, let's be reminded that it's not only the words that are spoken that hurt us.

Sometimes it is those words you long to hear, but perhaps never have, that are the most painful—the "I love you," or, "I'm proud of you." Words so simple yet spoken so seldom.

Words carry amazing power to bless or to curse. Listen to what the president of a leading pharmaceutical laboratory says: "My father was a country doctor. We now know, scientifically speaking, that he did not carry a thing in that black bag that could cure anybody. But people got well because he patted them on the back and said, 'You're going to make it.' That little bit of encouragement released the body's amazing power to heal itself."

This country doctor employed the practice of blessing with affirming words. He said to his sick patients: "You're going to make it." Every one of us desires to be encouraged…to be told that we are valued and loved.

The scene is the Jordan River. The occasion is the baptism of Jesus. As John the Baptist is baptizing Jesus, a voice is heard out of the heavens.

It is the voice of God. God the Father says of his son Jesus: "This is my Son in whom I am well pleased. What an awesome word of affirmation!

God the Father sets the example for all of us by speaking words of affirmation and affection for his Son! In these divine words Jesus is named, claimed, and ordained! Coming out of the Jordan River, Jesus begins his public ministry at the age of thirty. It is the Father's words of affirmation that provide inspiration for ministry!

As a believer in Christ, never forget the significance of your baptism! In a Service of Christian Baptism the baptized person's name is always called out—for in and through Jesus Christ we are named and find our identity now and forever! In a Service of Christian Baptism the baptized are always welcomed into the church fellowship—for Jesus claims us as his very own. And, in a Service of Christian Baptism the baptized are always challenged to faithful service to God and neighbor—for Jesus ordains every Christian as a minister!

Words. Words that name. Words that claim. Words that ordain.

As you take inventory of your relationships, how are you doing in the area of giving words of affirmation?

Are you taking others for granted, or are you granting them words of approval and affection?

Are you showing and telling them that you love them?

I was with a man recently who just wishes his deceased son was here so that he could share with him some affirming words. But it is now too late. The opportunity has passed.

God has given us the ultimate affirming words: "For God so loved the world that he gave his only begotten Son that whoever believes in him should not perish but have everlasting life" (John 3:16).

What awesome, affirming words to hear from our Creator—the One who names us, claims us, and ordains us for Christian service.

Now, as we are loved and affirmed, and given words of affirmation by our Lord, let us share words of loving affirmation and admiration with others in our journey of life.

PRAYER: O God, Name above all names, we praise you for naming, claiming, and ordaining us! We are your children. Once we were nobody, but now, through your acceptance and claiming we are somebody! In our baptism, you call us by name. You have us carved in the palm of your hand. You carry a "picture" of each of Your children! Through your loving deeds and gracious words we are affirmed.

Through your holy Son Christ we bear your name—Christians. Through your Holy Spirit we are enabled and empowered (ordained) to be ministers in Jesus' name. May we never forget the marvelous and miraculous truth that you know us and call us by name! In Christ's name, Amen.

QUESTIONS AND REFLECTIONS

1. How did you get your name? Do you know what your name actually means? List some names of which you know the meaning.

2. In what ways do names and words carry meaning and power?

3. Are there words that you long to hear from a significant other? Are there words that you withhold from a significant other in your life? Why?

4. Discuss the naming, claiming, and ordaining that occurs at Jesus' baptism in the Jordan River. Refer to Luke 3:21-22.

26

PINING FOR PATIENCE

"Be patient, then, brothers and sisters, until the Lord's coming. See how the farmer waits for the land to yield its valuable crops and how patient he is for the autumn and the spring rains" (James 5:7).

Growing Christmas trees is not for the impatient. In an age of instant gratification and quick results, raising fraser firs does not conform to the rapid race and pace.

Counting the time in the tree bed and growing time in the field, it could be ten to twelve or more years before a six to seven-foot tree is ready for harvest. The grower must patiently spend many years tending, shaping, and caring for the trees before there is a finished product. Through patience seedlings are nurtured into mature trees.

And, so, through patience Christian character is developed. This character shaping is not an event. It is not instantaneous. It is a process.

God invites us to participate in this process of character shaping! In the words of a Sunday school song: "He's still working on me, to make me what I ought to be. It took Him just a week to make the moon and the stars, the Sun and the Earth and Jupiter and Mars. How loving and patient He must be. He's still working on me!

God has a plan for our lives. The question for us is: "Is God's plan our plan?" And, is God's timing our timing? We become disobedient and ultimately disillusioned when we do not seek God's plan and God's timing. Instead, impatiently and rebelliously going our own way in our own time.

When things do not go our way. When the timing is not our timing, how impatient and immature we can often be! Which can sometimes lead us to being insensitive and harsh with others.

According to a traditional Hebrew story, Abraham was sitting outside his tent one evening when he saw an old man, weary from age and journey, coming toward him. Abraham rushed out, greeted him, and then invited him into his tent. There he washed the old man's feet and gave him food and drink.

The old man immediately began eating without saying any prayer or blessing. So Abraham asked him, "Don't you worship God?"

The older traveler replied, "I worship fire only and reverence no other god."

When he heard this, Abraham became incensed, grabbed the old man by the shoulders, and threw him out of his tent into the cold night air.

When the old man had departed, God called to his friend Abraham and asked where the stranger was. Abraham replied, "I forced him out because he did not worship you."

God answered, "I have suffered him these eighty years although he dishonors me. Could you not endure him one night?"

We set our agendas. We push our plans. We tout our timetables. Yet, carefully crafted agendas, best-laid plans, and set schedules often do not materialize just like we wish. And, when the unexpected occurs do we have a faith that affirms "God will make a way even though it may not be my way"?

May we learn a lesson from a short story entitled: "Three Trees in the Woods".

Once there were three trees on a hill in the woods. They were discussing their hopes and dreams when the first tree said, "Some day I hope to be a treasure chest. I could be filled with gold, silver, and precious gems. I could be decorated with intricate carving and everyone would see my beauty."

Then the second tree said, "Some day I will be a mighty ship. I will take kings and queens across the waters and sail to the corners of the world. Everyone will feel safe in me because of the strength of my hull."

Finally the third tree said, "I want to grow to be the tallest and straightest tree in the forest. People will see me on top of the hill and look up to my branches, and think of the heavens and God and how close to them I am reaching. I will be the greatest tree of all time and people will always remember me."

After a few years of praying their dreams would come true, a group of woodsmen came upon the trees. When one came to the first tree he said, "This looks like a strong tree, I think I should be able to sell the wood to a carpenter," and he began cutting it down. The tree was happy, because he knew that the carpenter would make him into a treasure chest.

At the second tree the woodsman said, "This looks like a strong tree, I should be able to sell it to the shipyard." The second tree was happy because he knew he was on his way to becoming a mighty ship.

When the woodsman came to the third tree, the tree was frightened because he knew if they cut him down his dreams would not come true. One of the woodsmen said, "I don't need anything special from my tree, so I'll take this one," and he cut it down.

When the first tree arrived at the carpenters, he was made into a feed box for animals. He was then placed in a barn and filled with hay. This was not at all what he had prayed for. The second tree was cut and made into a small fishing boat. His dreams of being a mighty ship and carrying kings had come to an end. The third tree was cut into large pieces and left alone in the dark.

The years went by, and the trees forgot about their dreams. Then one day, a man and woman came to the barn. She gave birth and they placed the baby in the hay in the feed box that was made from the first tree. The man wished that he could have made a crib for the baby, but this manger would have to do. The tree could feel the importance of this event and knew that it held the greatest treasure of all time.

Years later, a group of men got in the fishing boat made from the second tree. One of them was tired and went to sleep. While they were out on the water, a great storm arose and the tree didn't think it was strong enough to keep the men safe. The men woke the sleeping man, and He stood and said "Peace" and the storm stopped. At this moment, the tree knew that it had carried the King of kings in its boat.

Finally, someone came and got the third tree. It was carried through the streets as the people mocked the man who was carrying it. When they came to a stop, the man was nailed to the tree and raised in the air to die at the top of a hill. When Sunday came, the tree came to realize that it was strong enough to stand at the top of the hill and be as close to God as was possible, because Jesus had been crucified upon it.

When things don't seem to be going your way, always know that God has a plan for you. If you place your trust in Him, He will give you great gifts.

Each of the trees got what they wanted, just not in the way they had imagined. We don't always know what God's plans are for us. We just know that His ways are not our ways, but His ways are best.

Be patient…keep the faith. God has an awesome plan for your life!

We must stay the course in season and out of season. Just as there will come "spring times" in our lives, so also will come the "winters." May we allow the warm sun and abundant rains of Spring time to nurture our growth. And, may we permit the necessary waiting of the winter season to lend us rest and reflection so that we may gain proper perspective and godly wisdom for our days. Waiting can bring insight and build character.

Shortly after starting her perfume business, Estee Lauder realized she had to persuade a cosmetics buyer to place her products in many stores throughout the country.

At 9 A.M., Lauder was in the offices of the American Merchandising Corporation, waiting to see Marie Weston, the cosmetics buyer. Since Lauder had no appointment, she was advised to come back another day.

"I don't mind waiting," said Lauder. "I'll wait until she has a few free moments."

Salespeople came and went. At lunchtime, the receptionist said Weston's schedule was so full that getting in to see her was impossible. Again, Lauder was told to come back later.

"I'll wait a little longer," she persisted.

Hours passed. At 5:14 P.M. Marie Weston came out of her office. She looked at Estee Lauder in disbelief, then admiration, and said, "Well, do come in. Such patience must be rewarded."

Weston was impressed with Lauder's cosmetics, but there was no room in any of the stores. Come back later, she was encouraged. Of course, Estee did. Eventually, Weston found room in several stores. Business began to boom. The Estee Lauder name became famous in the world of cosmetics.

What "wall" are you up against in your life? Whatever it is, remember that God has a plan for your life and He will make a way, even when there seems to be no way! Wait patiently and persevere faithfully and sometime, somewhere a door will open.

James 5:7,8 instructs us with these words of encouragement: "Meanwhile, friends, wait patiently for the Master's Arrival. You see farmers do this all the time, waiting for their valuable crops to mature, patiently letting the rain do its slow but sure work. Be patient like that. Stay steady and strong..." (The Message).

If we will not give up and give out in our waiting goals and dreams will be fulfilled.

During my time of meditation I frequently include a writing by one of the great saints of the Christian tradition—St. Teresa of Avila. She speaks in this writing of the importance and necessity of patience:

> "Let nothing frighten you.
> Let nothing upset you.

> Everything is changing.
> God alone is changeless.
> Patience attains the goal.
> They who have God have everything.
> God alone supplies all our needs.

In our waiting it is important that we remain focused and trusting upon God! This is not waiting just for the sake of waiting. Rather, it is waiting with a purpose. Waiting with a God-provided goal.

We get caught up going in a myriad of directions and no longer focused and centered upon the most needed. So, in our waiting we must remain focused upon the essential so that we may be ready to move ahead when God calls. Not being pulled in all directions, but staying the course steady and strong.

Some years ago a speedboat driver who had survived a racing accident described what had happened. He said he had been at near top speeds when his boat veered slightly and hit a wave at a dangerous angle. The combined force of his speed and the size and angle of the wave sent the boat spinning crazily into the air. He was thrown from his seat and propelled deeply into the water—so deep, in fact, that he had no idea which direction the surface was. He had to remain calm and wait for the buoyancy of his life vest to begin pulling him up. Once he discovered which way was up, he could swim for the surface.

Sometimes we find ourselves surrounded by confusing options and choices, too deeply immersed in our problems to know which way is up. When this happens, we too can remain calm, waiting for God's gentle tug to pull us in the proper direction. Our "life vest" may be other Christians, Scripture, or some other leading from the Holy Spirit, but the key is recognizing our dependency upon God and trusting him.

And, as we stay focused upon the very best in life—loving God and loving people—let us persevere with patient hope. For the best is yet to come. So, let us not grow weary through the changing "Seasons" of life. Because each and every season of our life provides an opportunity for growth and maturity.

As I strolled through a field of mature Christmas trees, I was reminded of a "planting paradox." On the one hand, it seemed like these nine years of growing and trimming, and caring for these trees had taken forever! On the other hand, it just seemed like yesterday that these 6 to 7 foot beautiful frasers had been small seedlings just placed in the soil.

Patiently and consistently, attending to the basic growing and nurturing needs of these trees, month after month, and year after year, had resulted in strong,

healthy, beautiful Christmas trees. The patience practiced in the planting, cultivating, and growing paid off at the harvest!

PRAYER: O Patient, Heavenly Parent, thank you for not giving up on us!
You have designed us with purpose to our days. Help us to discover your purpose
for us and during those times when the purpose is not so clear empower us to
patiently wait upon your will.

During our most confusing seasons, Lord, enable us more than ever to stay
centered and focused upon you, affirming that as we remain focused upon you
patience will attain the goal!

QUESTIONS AND REFLECTIONS

1. Recount the story of Abraham related in chapter 29. In what ways is our patience with each other based upon God's grace shown to us?

2. What does the short story, "Three Trees in the Woods" say to you about providential care and human patience?

3. Meditate upon St. Teresa of Avila's writing. Recall a difficult season in your life, perhaps currently. How do St. Teresa's words speak to your situation?

4. Read and discuss James 5:7-8.

27

AIN'T NOTHING LIKE THE REAL THING, BABY

"You're hopeless, you religion scholars and Pharisees! Frauds! You burnish the surface of your cups and bowls so they sparkle in the sun, while the insides are maggoty with your greed and gluttony. Stupid Pharisees! Scour the insides, and then the gleaming surface will mean something" (Matthew 23:25,26, The Message).

One Advent-Christmas Season a number of years ago, after I had exited the Christmas tree growing enterprise, I decided to surprise my family by purchasing and bringing home an artificial Christmas tree. It did surprise them, but not in the manner I had hope to surprise them!

I thought, you see, that the artificial tree would make it easier and cleaner. No more pine needles all over. No more tree leaning, or worse yet falling in the living room in the middle of the night! Easy set up. Easy clean up.

Well, you would have thought the family pet died, or some other tragic event had occurred!

My wife and children were not happy campers. They expressed to me in no uncertain terms that they wanted a real tree, not an artificial tree. They missed the smell of a live evergreen, and the look, and even the mess of the pine needles, they claimed, made it seem more like Christmas. But, instead, I was the scrooge that had supplied them with some plastic, factory-manufactured Christmas tree complete with sections that were inserted into one another. Needless to say, that was our first...and last...artificial Christmas tree!

How often we opt, or settle, for the artificial instead of the real. How many times have we longed to be real with someone, and, instead, end up pretending and putting on a front once again!

Research psychologists have found there are at least three situations when we do not act like ourselves. First, the average person puts on airs when he visits the lobby of a fancy hotel. Next, the typical Jane Doe will try to hide her emotions and fake the salesperson when she enters the new-car showroom. And finally, as we take our seat in church or synagogue, we try to fool the Almighty into thinking that we have been good all week.

Pretension is poison. Deception is deadly. And faking your way through life leads to futility and ultimately to failure.

The Pharisees of Jesus' day—religious leaders and protectors of the Law—were notorious for their self-righteousness! They were quick to point out others' flaws but slow to admit their own weaknesses. In the twenty-third chapter of Matthew's Gospel Jesus gives these Pharisaic pretenders a scathing lecture: "Woe to you, teachers of the law and Pharisees, you hypocrites! You are like whitewashed tombs, which look beautiful on the outside but on the inside are full of dead men's bones and everything unclean. In the same way, on the outside you appear to people as righteous but on the inside you are full of hypocrisy and wickedness" (Matthew 23:27,28, NIV).

These experts in the Jewish Mosaic Law attempted to fake their way through life. But Jesus saw right through the pretension and called them on the carpet! Trying to be someone or something you are not is a losing and disillusioning path to take. And, besides that, you cannot fool God.

God doesn't ask us for perfection, he asks us for reflection—to reflect his love and grace to others. God doesn't call us to be successful; God calls us to be faithful. God wants us to escape hypocrisy and embrace integrity. We may appear perfect and faithful and avoiding hypocrisy to some people—to those who do not know us very well—But, to the One who made us, we can never get away with faking it! He knows our thoughts and our motives.

How do you get a great parking space at a New York Yankees baseball game? One man thought he had a way. According to the Fresno, California "Bee," this man pulled his car into the VIP parking lot and casually informed the attendant that he was a friend of George Steinbrenner, owner of the Yankees. Unfortunately for the imposter, the person attending the parking lot that day was George Steinbrenner himself, doing some personal investigation of traffic problems at the stadium.

The surprised imposter looked at Steinbrenner and said, "Guess I've got the wrong lot." You can be sure that he did not park in the VIP lot that day or ever.

The owner knows his friends. The owner determines who gets in the VIP lot. God also knows who his friends are and who the imposters are.

Certainly there are risks that come with being real and authentic. You may not get a VIP parking space. You may have persons laugh at you and ridicule you for being real. But, there is such liberation and joy that comes with authenticity—for we are being who God has intended us to be!

Authenticity is not the easy path, but it is the only meaningful path. For it is the path that acknowledges: "I cannot go this thing of life on my own…I need God's help and the help of others along the way."

One father describes vulnerability this way:

"The speech was finished and the audience had been generous with its applause, and in the car on the way home my 14-year-old son turned to me and said: 'I really admire you, Dad, being able to get up there and give a speech like that. You always know, what to say to people. You always seem to know what you're doing.'

I smiled when he said that. I may even have blushed modestly. But, at that moment, I didn't know what to say at all.

After a while I thanked him and assured him that some day he would be comfortable speaking in front of an audience, that he would always know what to say to people, that he would always know what he was doing. But what I really wanted to say to my son was that his father was not at all what he appeared to be and that being a man is frequently a facade.

It has taken me a long time to admit that—even to myself. Especially to myself. My father, after all, really had always known what he was doing. He was strong and confident and he never felt pain, never knew fear. There wasn't a leaky faucet he couldn't fix or an engine he couldn't manage to get running again. Mechanics never fooled him, salesmen never conned him. He was always calm in emergencies, always cool under fire. He never cried.

For a long time I wondered how such a man could have produced such a weakling for a son. I wondered where the self-doubts and the fears I felt all the time had come from. I wondered why the faucets I fixed always dripped twice as fast after I got finished with them, why engines that sputtered before I started to work on them went stone-dead under my wrench. I dreaded the thought, that some day my father would see me cry. I didn't realize that fathers are not always everything they seem to be.

It's different for fathers than it is for mothers. Motherhood is honest, close to the surface. Mothers don't have to hide what they feel. They don't have to pretend.

When there are sounds downstairs in the middle of the night, a mother is allowed to pull the covers over her head and hope that they will go away. A father is supposed to put on his slippers and robe and march boldly down the stairs, even if he's pretty sure that it's the Manson family waiting for him in the kitchen.

When the road signs are confusing and the scenery is starting to look awfully unfamiliar, it's perfectly natural for a mother to pull over to the side of the road and ask for directions from the first person who comes along. A father is supposed to know exactly where he's going, even if he has to drive 200 miles out of the way to prove it.

Mothers can bang a new jar of peanut butter on the floor until the lid is loose enough to turn. Fathers are supposed to twist it off with their bare hands—without getting red in the face.

Mothers who lose their jobs are unfortunate. Fathers who lose their jobs are failures.

When a mother gets hurt she may want to swear, but she is only allowed to cry. When a father gets hurt he may want to cry, but he is only allowed to swear...

I should have told him that the only reason his father, like lots of fathers, doesn't admit his weaknesses is because he's afraid that someone will think he is not a real man.

More important, what I should have said to my 14-year-old son in the car that night is that someday, when he's a father, he'll feel fear and self-doubt and pain, and that is all right. But my father never told me, and I haven't told my son." (D. L. Stewart, "Why Fathers Hide Their Feelings," Redbook, January 1985, p. 32).

Whenever I go up in our attic, and look way back in the corner, I usually spot our artificial Christmas tree, used only once, and probably never to be used at our home again—because we have opted for the real instead of the artificial.

PRAYER: Holy God, may we come before you acknowledging our brokenness and seeking your wholeness. Help us to be real in a world of false impressions. Help us to choose authenticity in a world of complicity. And, help us to choose the path of integrity, not hypocrisy. In the name of the only true and good Savior we pray, Amen.

QUESTIONS AND REFLECTIONS

1. According to the research psychologists' studies there are at least three situations when we do not act like ourselves. Do you agree with these three? Are there other situations?

2. Review Matthew 23:27-28. Read more of Matthew, chapter 23, looking for Jesus' confrontation of the self-righteous Pharisees. What do you discover about the Pharisees? What do you discover about yourself?

3. Explain and respond to this chapter quotation: "God doesn't ask us for perfection, he asks us for reflection—to reflect his love and grace to others."

4. What do you take as the main message(s) of the story of the father and the 14-year-old son?

28

HARVEST TIME

"Now learn this lesson from the fig tree: As soon as its twigs get tender and its leaves come out, you know that summer is near. Even so, when you see all these things, you know that it is near, right at the door. I tell you the truth, this generation will certainly not pass away until all these things have happened. Heaven and earth will pass away, but my words will never pass away"—Jesus (Matthew 24:32-35).

Harvesting Christmas trees is no picnic. In fact, it's hard labor. The trees must be selected and cut and dragged and bailed and loaded.

But not only is harvesting time a time of physical perspiration it is also a time of great emotional celebration. After years of tending the trees it is gratifying to behold the finished product. Each tree is unique. Each tree has its own special beauty. And each tree bears its flaws—identifying marks of genetics and environmental influences.

The trees considered suitable for harvesting—those ready for the Christmas tree market—are evaluated, measured, and then color-coded, with various colors of adhesive tape. For example, red might identify a 6-7 foot fraser fir. Blue could mark a 7-8 foot tree, and so on.

Harvest time usually begins in November—which provides about four to six weeks to get the work done in time for Christmas.

Considering what goes on the rest of the years, harvesting time is a relatively short window of time. The grower wants the trees to be as fresh and green as possible; yet also ample time to ship to distant locations in time for the holiday season. Therefore there are a lot of long, hard days during harvest time.

Proverbs 10:5 reminds us: "At harvest season it's smart to work hard, but stupid to sleep." Implied here is the message that we must work hard, and not faint, because the harvest time is upon us…and there is much to be done.

Matthew tells us in his gospel: "Jesus went to every town and village…teaching in their synagogues and preaching the gospel of the kingdom, and healing every disease and every infirmity. When he saw the crowds, he had compassion for them, because they were harassed and helpless, like sheep without a shepherd. Then he said to his disciples, 'The harvest is plentiful, but the laborers are few; pray therefore the Lord of harvest to send out laborers into his harvest.'"

We live in an age in which many people are "shepherdless". They are lost. They have no direction. They are trapped in an endless existential existence. Symptoms of this quiet desperation include loneliness, futility and emptiness. Seeking to eradicate these wounds, our culture runs to the captivating cadence of bigger, more, faster and busier!

In our lonely, isolated drivenness there is very little "harvest activity" because we are so consumed and directed by our own desires, hurts, and interests. If this attitude and posture toward life goes unabated and uninterrupted we too are in danger of being counted among the "harassed and helpless" of whom Jesus speaks.

What we thought would satisfy and comfort, ironically leads to our own disillusioning demise. For "we all like sheep have gone astray. We have each gone our own way." We have each set our own parameters. We have played by our own rules. And, we have established our own standards.

When fraser firs are selected for harvest time, the Christmas tree farmer carries a measuring stick—a standard of length (a canon)—to determine which trees meet the harvest requirement. The farmer sets the standard. Only the trees that measure up will qualify.

An armed robber by the name of Dennis Lee Curtis was arrested in 1992 in Rapid City, South Dakota. Curtis apparently had scruples about his thievery. In his wallet the police found a sheet of paper on which was written the following code:

1. I will not kill anyone unless I have to.

2. I will not take cash and food stamps—no checks.

3. I will rob only at night.

4. I will not wear a mask.

5. I will not rob mini-marts or 7-Eleven stores.

6. If I get chased by cops on foot, I will get away. If chased by vehicle, I will not put the lives of innocent civilians on the line.

7. I will rob only seven months out of the year.

8. I will enjoy robbing from the rich to give to the poor.

This thief had a sense of morality, but it was flawed. When he stood before the court, he was not judged by the standards he had set for himself but by the higher law of the state. (Brian Burrell, "Words We Live By"; S & S Trade, 1997).

Likewise, when we stand before God, we will not be judged by the code and standard of life we have written for ourselves, but by God's perfect and righteous standard. And there is no way we can measure up to God's high and holy standards, for God's ways are not our ways.

Yet the beautiful and merciful reality is that the Almighty Judge, the Holy Harvester, offers us abundant and eternal life, beginning here and now and never ending!

Through the crucifixion-resurrection event, God, through Jesus Christ, has graciously and lovingly paid the price for our sinfulness. Perfect divinity has made a way for flawed humanity.

And as we place our faith and trust in Jesus' gracious forgiveness, we experience at-one-ment (atonement) with God our Creator. How wonderful to look into the eyes of our Almighty Judge only to see our all-loving Savior!

But, it does not end here. Because God blesses us to be a blessing to others. As we receive, we give. As we are forgiven, we forgive. As we are recipients of Christ's mercy, so too do we show mercy to our neighbor.

In this way, we become agents of change for God in our lives and in the lives of others. As you claim and proclaim this divine gift of positive and powerful faith it is absolutely amazing what God can and will do!

Sometimes we are afforded the high privilege of watching a "seedling" grow to be a strong, mature "tree". Yet, more often it seems we plant seeds or water plants alongside the work of other folk. And even though we may not see the results we desire, nor the fruit we had hoped for; nonetheless, when done in Jesus' name our efforts are not without reward and our lives are not without joy as we realize God is somehow employing ourselves and our gifts in His eternal creation!

Our joy becomes more complete, then, as our focus becomes more God-centered rather than ego-centric. Or, as the words of a colloquialism state: "We need to take ourselves less seriously and God more seriously."

We each have unique and wonderful gifts to be used on this earth…but only because the Gift-Giver has bestowed these gifts upon us; developed them within us; and graciously used them in His kingdom work.

St. Paul expresses this idea of a God-centered lifestyle in his letter to the Corinthian Christians:

"What, after all, is Apollos? And what is Paul? Only servants, through whom you came to believe—as the Lord has assigned to each his task. I planted the seed, Apollos watered it, but God made it grow. So neither he who plants nor he who waters is anything, but only God, who makes things grow. The man who plants and the man who waters have one purpose, and each will be rewarded according to his own labor. For we are God's fellow workers; you are God's field, God's building.

By the grace God has given me, I laid a foundation as an expert builder, and someone else is building on it. But each one should be careful how he builds. For no one can lay any foundation other than the one already laid, which is Jesus Christ."

The harvesting…the "fruit" of the harvest…the results of the harvest…is not about us. It's about God! The life we have. The resources we possess. The gifts we exemplify. They all belong to God. And God graciously allows us to participate in his kingdom work flawed though we are!

A house servant had two large pots. One hung on each end of a pole that he carried across his neck. One of the pots had a crack in it. At the end of the long walk from the stream to the master's house, the cracked pot arrived only half full. The other pot was perfect and always delivered a full portion of water.

For two years the servant delivered each day only one-and-a-half pots of full water to his master's house. The perfect pot was proud of its accomplishments, but the poor cracked pot was ashamed of its own imperfection, and miserable over accomplishing only half of what it had been made to do.

After two years of what it perceived to be bitter failure, the cracked pot spoke to the servant one day by the stream.

"I am ashamed of myself, and I want to apologize to you."

"What are you ashamed of?" asked the bearer.

"For these past two years I have been able to deliver only half my load because this crack in my side causes water to leak out all the way to your master's house. Because of my flaws, you don't get full value from your work."

The servant said, "As we return to the master's house, I want you to notice the beautiful flowers along the path." As they went up the hill, the cracked pot noticed the beautiful wild flowers on the side of the path. When they reached the house, the servant said to the pot, "Did you notice the flowers grew only on your side of the path, not on the other pot's side? That's because I have always known about your flaw, and I took advantage of it. I planted flower seeds on your side of the path, and every day while we walk back from the stream, you've watered them. For two years I have been able to pick beautiful flowers to decorate my master's table."

Each of us has flaws. But if we allow it, the Lord will use our flaws to grace his Father's table.

In attempting to do the Lord's work. In seeking to participate in the harvest, by reaching people with the good news of our Lord and Savior Jesus Christ...some will plant...some will water...but, it is God who brings the growth. And, by His amazing grace he uses us "warts and all"; flawed though we are, to participate in his harvest fields and to build his kingdom—on earth as it is in heaven!

We each have a part in God's harvest ministry. We all have the same purpose. While one may broadcast seed, another may water the seed...and it is all for the same goal—"For we are God's fellow workers."

"...and each will be rewarded according to his own labor."

In our living, in our ministry, as we rely upon God's power and direction amazing results can and do happen!

A mother, hoping to reinforce her young son's progress at the piano, purchased tickets to a Paderewski concert. When the night arrived, they located their seats near the front of the concert hall, impressed by the elegant Steinway waiting on stage.

The mother soon found a friend to talk to, and the boy slipped away. At eight o'clock the spotlights came on, and the audience quieted. Only then did the mother notice her son on the piano bench, innocently playing "Twinkle, Twinkle, Little Star."

The mother was frantic; but before she could intervene, the master appeared on stage and quickly moved to the keyboard.

"Don't quit—Keep playing," he whispered to the boy. Leaning over, Paderewski reached down with his left hand and began filling in a bass part. Soon his right arm reached around the other side, encircling the child, to add a running obbligato. Together, the old master and the young novice held the crowd mesmerized.

In our lives, unpolished though they may be, it is the Master who surrounds us and whispers in our ear, time and time again, "Don't quit—Keep playing."

And as we do, he augments and supplements until a work of amazing beauty is created.

God has placed within the Body of Christ, the Church, the seeds of justice and peace. The question remains, will these seeds of justice and peace find receptivity and growth in fertile, pliable soil, or will they find a hard and rocky soil—resistant to gospel harvest?

Before Jesus of Nazareth left this earth and ascended to be seated at the right hand of God the Father Almighty, he left us with a harvest commission—called the Great Commission:

"All authority in heaven and on earth has been given to me. Therefore, go and make disciples of all nations, baptizing them in the name of the Father and of Son and of the Holy Spirit, and teaching them to obey everything I have commanded you. And surely I am with you always, to the very end of the age" (Matthew 28:18-20).

Every believer is to lend a hand in helping the harvest ministry of Christ. Like the young novice on the piano, bringing what we have to offer, and the Master comes along side and magnifies and multiplies the gift. In the final analysis we are not responsible for the response of our sisters and brothers. We will, however, be held accountable for our response.

Furthermore, our rewards, much like the harvested Christmas trees, will not be based upon our own criteria and standards, but upon God's standards.

Our standards always fall short of God's standards. Our efforts fall short of God's expectations. And our best laid plans and intentions are riddled with shortcomings and inadequacies.

But thanks be to Jesus Christ who stands in our place before God, the supreme Judge, and pleads our case and takes our place so that we may find forgiveness, healing, and reconciliation with our Creator!

One person reflecting upon his last college exam for a tough logic class shared:

To help them on their test, the professor told them they could bring as much information to the exam as they could fit on a piece of notebook paper. Most students crammed as many facts as possible on their 81/2 X 11 inch sheet of paper.

But one student walked into class, put a piece of notebook paper on the floor, and had an advanced logic student stand on the paper. The advanced logic student told him everything he needed to know. He was the only student to receive an A.

The ultimate final exam will come when we stand before God and he asks, "Why should I let you in?" On our own we cannot pass that exam. But we have Someone who will stand in for us! Thanks be to God!

PRAYER: Heavenly Harvester, what a wonder that you have allowed us, your creation, to assist in your harvest ministry! Let us never forget that an act of mercy and a word of kindness can lead to eternal ramifications.

Dear Lord, we are so quick to play God in others' lives. We rush at separating the "wheat" and the "weeds", while your wise words remind and encourage us to keep planting seeds and let God be God in others' lives.

This harvest matter is about measuring up to your standards, Lord. Not my standards. Not my neighbor's standards. But, your divine, eternal standards.

In response to your great grace seen and experienced most completely in Jesus Christ, let us work diligently and consistently going about God's harvest ministry. Yet, acknowledging and recognizing all the while that even our very best falls short and we have need of an Advocate—none other than God's Son, our Savior, Jesus Christ—the One in whom we harvest and believe and pray. Amen.

QUESTIONS AND REFLECTIONS

1. Proverbs 10:5 relates: "At harvest season it's smart to work hard, but stupid to sleep." How does this relate to Christian evangelism?

2. Jesus tells his disciples: "The harvest is plentiful, but the laborers are few; pray, therefore, the Lord of harvest to send out laborers into his harvest." How do these words of Jesus have application for our lives today?

3. Respond to the following quotation: "We live in an age in which many people are "shepherdless". They are lost. They have no direction. They are trapped in an endless existential existence. Symptoms of this quiet desperation include loneliness, futility and emptiness."

4. "...When we stand before God, we will not be judged by the code and standard of life we have "written" for ourselves but by God's perfect standard." Discuss the validity and implications of this statement.

5. How does the following statement give you hope? "How wonderful to look into the eyes of our Almighty Judge only to see our all-loving Savior?

29

THE PLEASING AROMA OF THE PINES

"But thanks be to God, who always leads us in triumphal procession in Christ and through us spreads everywhere the fragrance of the knowledge of him. For we are to God the aroma of Christ among those who are being saved and those who are perishing" (II Corinthians 2:14-15).

To me, one of the most pleasing natural smells is that of the pine tree. During the shearing and harvesting times this alluring aroma is most abundant. Many people purchase a live pine tree for their home at Christmas time in order, for example, to enjoy the fragrance of a faser fir.

As Christians, our lives are to be the aroma of Christ unto God—as we follow Christ obediently—and a winning fragrance to the world around us. St. Paul writes: "But thanks be to God, who always leads us in triumphal procession in Christ and through us spreads everywhere the fragrance of the knowledge of him. For we are to God the aroma of Christ among those who are being saved and those who are perishing."

The pleasing, alluring aroma comes from faithfully, obediently following Christ. The fragrance of God overcomes hatred with love. The aroma of Christ disarms evil with good.

On April 6, 2000, Ricky and Toni Sexton were taken hostage inside their Wytheville, Virginia, home by a fugitive couple on a crime spree. Toni had taken her poodle outside when Dennis Lewis, 37, and Angela Tanner, 20, roared into her driveway, pointed pistols at her, and yelled at her to get back inside the house.

Inside the house, the Sextons turned their hostage experience into an opportunity to demonstrate Christian love. The Sextons listened to their captors' troubles, fed them, showed them gospel videos, read to them from the Bible, and prayed and cried with them.

During negotiations with the police, Ricky Sexton refused his own release when Lewis and Tanner suggested that they might end the standoff by committing suicide. The standoff had an unusual ending. Before surrendering to the police, Angela Tanner left $135 and a note for the Sextons that read: "Thank you for all your hospitality. We really appreciate it. I hope he gets better. Wish all luck and love. Please accept this. It really is all we have to offer. Love, Angela and Dennis." (The Roanoke Times; April 8, 2000; p.A-1).

Followers of Jesus should never forget the disarming power of the aroma of Jesus Christ's love!

In the hands of God, our everyday actions and attitudes become contagious fragrances that carry spiritual and eternal influence and power.

This contagious fragrance and alluring aroma is not produced in and of ourselves. It arrives as God through Christ lives within us. It derives from obedience to God. Scripture informs: "To obey is better than sacrifice."

In the Old Testament era Jewish worshipers of God would bring to the Temple, as part of their offering, sweet smelling incense (as well as animal sacrifice, crops, etc.)—But, at times, when the Jewish people were bringing all these offerings, yet they were not obedient to God—God rejected their incense offerings. God said these insincere incense offerings stink!

"Stop bringing meaningless offerings! Your incense is detestable to me..." (Isaiah 1:13a).

God desires our willing and loving service, not our legalistic law-keeping. God wants our obedience not a "Pharasaic performance".

Susan Maycinik writes: "The line between obedience and performance can be a blurry one. Yet it is an important distinction to grasp, because obedience leads to life, and performance to death...

Obedience is seeking God with your whole heart. Performance is having a quiet time because you'll feel guilty if you don't.

Obedience is finding ways to let the Word of God dwell in you richly. Performance is quickly scanning a passage so you can check it off your Bible reading plan.

Obedience is inviting guests to your home for dinner. Performance is feeling anxious about whether every detail of the meal will be perfect.

Obedience is following God's prompting to start a small group. Performance is reluctance to let anyone else lead the group because they might not do it as well as you would.

Obedience is doing your best. Performance is wanting to be the best.

Obedience is saying yes to whatever God asks of you. Performance is saying yes to whatever people ask of you.

Obedience is following the prompting of God's Spirit. Performance is following a list of human-made requirements.

Obedience springs from fear (respect) of God. Performance springs from fear of failure.

When we follow the path of obedience to God, and not the path of human performance, we become a wonderful and winsome divine aroma. Because we share the love and truth of God.

And, as we rub shoulders with the world we allow God's alluring aroma to be shared through our lives. Christians, then, become a refreshing fragrance, a contagious presence and a preserving seasoning.

. In his book, "Led By the Carpenter" (Thomas Nelson, 1999; p. 46), D. James Kennedy writes:

A man walked into a little mom-and-pop grocery store and asked, "Do you sell salt?"

"Ha!" said Pop the proprietor. "Do we sell salt! Just look!" And Pop showed the customer one entire wall of shelves stocked with nothing but salt—Morton salt, iodized salt, kosher salt, rock salt, garlic salt, seasoning salt, Epsom salts—every kind of salt imaginable.

"Wow!" said the customer.

"You think that's something?" said Pop with a wave of the hand.

"That's nothing! Come look." And Pop led the customer to a back room filled with shelves and bins and cartons and barrels and boxes of salt. "Do we sell salt!" he said.

"Unbelievable!" said the customer.

"You think that's something?" said Pop. "Come! I'll show you salt!"

And Pop led the customer down some steps into a huge basement, five times as large as the previous room, filled wall, floor, to ceiling, with every imaginable form and size and shape of salt—even huge ten-pound salt licks for the cow pasture.

"Incredible!" said the customer. "You really do sell salt!"

"No!" said Pop. "That's just the problem! We never sell salt! But that salt salesman—Hoo-boy! Does he sell salt!"

Salt that stays one the shelf doesn't do any good at all. So, too, the contagious, sweet-smelling aroma of God's love in our life is to be given away…put into action…not "stored on the shelf" doing no one any good!

The powerful fragrance of the good news of God in Jesus Christ ought to flow through our lives and emanate outward to others—not a negative, over-powering aroma, but a positive, pervasive and persuading perfume, much like the pleasing fragrance of a pine tree pleasantly permeating our homes at Christmas time.

PRAYER: Heavenly Father, the fragrance of your freeing good news is so appealing and contagious to our souls! Thank you! Yet, we sometimes run toward, and spread, that which stinks in your almighty and holy nostrils!

We have our hearts centered and focused on anything but you, yet we attempt to sugar-coat things with sacrifice and incense-burning. You have told us through you word: "To obey is better than sacrifice." You want us first and foremost. Because, as our loving heavenly Parent, you know that if you have us and our obedient faith, the sacrifices will follow in time.

God, help us to be obedient to you because you love us and you know what is best for us. And, if we are obedient to you and your word we can be assured that our life will be an appealing aroma that will point and lead others to Christ. In Christ's name we pray, Amen.

QUESTIONS AND REFLECTIONS

1. In this chapter we read: "As Christians, our lives are to be the aroma of Christ unto God—as we follow Christ obediently—and a winning fragrance to the world around us." Discuss the relationship of "the aroma of Christ unto God" and "a winning fragrance to the world". How are these two inter-related? Is one required before the other?

2. Scripture records: "To obey is better than sacrifice." What are your interpretations and reflections concerning this scripture?

3. What might be some of the differences between "path of obedience to God" and "human performance"? What might be some of the similarities of the two?

4. "The powerful fragrance of the good news of God in Jesus Christ ought to flow through our lives and emanate outwards to others—not a negative, over-powering aroma, but a positive, pervasive and persuading perfume..." Perfume on our bodies, not unlike salt poured on our food, can be pleasing when the right amount is applied. But, when it is overdone (or under done) there can be really negative consequences and responses. Explain.

30

THE GIVING TREE

"The Lord God put the man in the Garden of Eden to take care of it and to look after it" (Genesis 2:15).

Psalm of the Woodlands

As a tree in the forest becomes tall reaching for the light
may we grow above the shadows of sin, fear, and doubt.
As it gives shelter and shade to its friends of fur and feather,
so may we help those brothers and sisters
who are smaller and weaker than ourselves.
The tree sends down roots deep into the soil
that it may be nourished by mother earth.
May we be as firmly grounded by the love of Christ
and sustained by his grace.
If a tree falls and decays, it provides nourishment for new plants
and gives its place in the sun for others.
Our Lord and Savior died to make a new life and a new place for us.
When a tree in the forest is cut down,
its wood is used for shelter and fuel.
Jesus taught that only when life is surrendered,
when love is poured out,
can we build his kingdom and reflect the warmth of his Spirit. Amen.

—(Milton Vahey, U.S.A., 20th century—The United Methodist Book of Worship; The United Methodist Publishing House, Nashville, TN. P. 508)

Using a live Christmas tree in your home during the holidays can actually help the environment. Real trees help the environment from the time they are planted in the field until after Christmas, when they can be recycled.

While growing, Christmas trees support life by absorbing carbon dioxide and other harmful gases while providing fresh oxygen. Every acre of Christmas trees planted gives off enough oxygen to meet the needs of eighteen people. Today in America there are enough Christmas trees planted that approximately eighteen million people a day are supplied with oxygen!

In addition, trees grown on Christmas tree farms stabilize soil, protect water supplies, and provide a refuge for wildlife while creating a beautiful scenic view. Very often Christmas trees are planted in soil that will not support other crops. So, the trees help utilize the land...furthering good stewardship of the earth. And, when one tree is cut down, one or two are replanted in its place.

Furthermore, after the Christmas tree's beautiful looks and pleasant aroma have been enjoyed it can serve another positive purpose—it is recyclable. The branches and trunk are biodegradable and can be transformed into mulch for the garden and yard. A Christmas tree placed in the back yard will make a functional bird feeder and the birds may also employ the tree branches for shelter during the winter winds. Large quantities of trees make effective barriers on beaches to prevent soil erosion. Sunk into ponds, the trees will also make an excellent refuge and feeding area for fish.

In the scheme of strong stewardship Christmas trees play a vital and important role. These trees not only give...they give life.

One of my favorite children's stories is The Giving Tree by author Shel Silverstein. (Harper and Row, Publishers; New York, Evanston, and London; 1964)

The Giving Tree relates the story of a tree's relationship with a little boy. Everyday the little boy would play on the tree. He would gather leaves and make a pretend king's crown. He would climb up the tree's trunk, swing from her branches, and eat her fruit. When the boy was sleepy from playing so hard he would sleep in the tree's shade. The boy loved the tree very much and this made the tree happy.

But as the boy grew older the tree felt deserted by its friend. One day the boy approached the tree and the tree said, "Come, boy, come and climb up my trunk and swing from my branches and eat apples and play in my shade and be happy."

"I am too big to climb and play," said the boy. "I want to buy things and have fun. I want some money. Can you give me some money?"

"I'm sorry," said the tree, "but I have no money. I have only leaves and apples. Take my apples, boy, and sell them in the city. Then you will have money and you will be happy."

The boy picked the apples and carried them away to sell. And this made the tree very happy.

The boy, again, stayed away for a long time. Then one day the boy returned…this time as a grown man who wished for a house to shelter his wife and family.

"Can you give me a house?"

"I have no house," said the tree.

"The forest is my house, but you may cut off my branches and build a house. Then you will be happy."

So the man cut off the tree's branches and carried them away to build his house.

The next time the man returned he was old and tired of life. The tree invited him to play. But the man said he was too sad to play. "I want a boat that will take me far away from here. Can you give me a boat."

And the tree offered its trunk to be made into a boat. And so the man cut down the tree trunk, made a boat, and sailed away.

Finally, after a long, long time the man returned to the tree. "I am sorry, boy," said the tree, "but I have nothing left to give you."

After all, the apples were gone. The branches were gone. The trunk was gone. But that was alright with the old man for all he needed was a place to sit and rest. The old stump made a perfect seat for the tired man. And so he sat and rested. And the tree was once again very happy.

God has provided for us in so many ways. A gracious and giving God made even the "giving" trees so that we may have an abundance of oxygen, apples, wood for homes, and even gorgeous autumn leaves. God's natural creation is brimming with beauty and abundance! We ought to do all within our power to lovingly care for this wonderful planet on which we are blessed to reside.

When the first two human beings were created, God placed them in a garden and instructed them to "take care of it and look after it."

Those are still our instructions today, perhaps even more so now with the way we have neglected to care for the earth. Let us lovingly tend to the world God has entrusted to our care.

PRAYER: Creator God, you have provided for all our needs. You have entrusted us with so very much!! There are enough resources for all peoples if only we would lovingly care for your earth and compassionately share with all in need. Give us eyes to more completely see your nurturing care in the beauty of a flower, your grace-filled manner in the acceptance of a pet, and your giving and gracious nature in even the provisions of a tree. Amen.

QUESTIONS AND REFLECTIONS

1. Read again The Giving Tree as recounted in this chapter. What does this story have to tell us about human reliance upon natural resources?

2. What are some everyday, simple ways we can all practice good stewardship of God's earth?

3. When Adam and Eve were placed in the Garden, they were instructed by the Creator to "take care of it and look after it." If you were to issue a report card to humankind grading us on our care and stewardship of the earth, what would be our grade? Why?

ABOUT THE AUTHOR

Michael D. Kurtz is an elder in the Western North Carolina Conference of The United Methodist Church. He is married to Karen Christy Kurtz and they have two children—Joshua and Anna. He holds an Associate of Arts degree from Lees McRae College, a Bachelor of Arts from Eastern Mennonite University, a Master of Divinity degree from Duke Divinity School, and a Doctor of Ministry degree with an emphasis on marriage and family ministries from Eastern Baptist Theological Seminary.

Michael enjoys reading, playing basketball and golf, playing guitar, swimming, yard work, and writing. He also works part time as a licensed marriage and family therapist.

Other published writings by Rev. Kurtz include: Various articles for Graded Press, including "Everyday Life in the Times of the Judges"—included in Abingdon's "Bible Teacher Kit"; co-authored the book "Approaching the New Millennium: Biblical End-Time Images"; Wrote the Adult Bible Studies Teacher Manual for Spring of 1991; Michael and his wife Karen have also produced a musical CD ("Friends for Life") in which eight of their own original songs are featured.

0-595-33225-0

Made in the USA
Lexington, KY
08 January 2012